Collected Works of
Professor B. R. Grover
Vol. VI

Zamindars and Jagirdars in the Mughal Age

Collected Works of
Professor B. R. Grover
Vol. VI

Zamindars and Jagirdars in the Mughal Age

Edited by

Miss Amrita Grover
Dr. Anju Grover Chaudhary
Dr. J.C. Dua

Originals
Delhi-110052

First Published 2012

ISBN 81-8454-109-0
ISBN 978-81-8454-109-0 (Vol. 6)

Published by
Originals
A-6, Nimri Commercial Centre,
Ashok Vihar Phase-IV, Delhi-110052
Phones: 011-27302453, Fax: 011-47061936
e-mail: info@Lppindia.com
visit us at: www.Lppindia.com

Printed at
D K Fine Art Press P Ltd.
Delhi-110052

PRINTED IN INDIA

Dedicated to the Memory of my Esteemed Brother Professor B.R. Grover

Amrita Grover

Table of Contents

About the Author

(b. 1923- d. 2001)

Professor B.R. Grover, former Chairman of the Indian Council of Historical Research, with an academic and administrative career spanning more than 55 years, has left an indelible mark as one of India's most eminent and dedicated historians. He has left behind a massive wealth of historical research based on original Persian, Urdu, Ottoman Turkish, Punjabi and English sources. Known for doing intensive research in the archives and libraries of India, several European countries and the United States of America, Professor Grover had carved out a distinct position for himself as a moving encyclopaedia of source material on agrarian history of the Mughals, especially the land revenue administration.

Upon his death on May 10, 2001, the then Prime Minister Atal Behari Vajpayee paid him a rich tribute, stating: šHe would always be remembered for his formidable legacy of excellence, erudition, and dedication to historical research and academic administration.› Dr. Murli Manohar Joshi, then Minister of Human Resources and Scientific Research, paid him a personal homage and called him a real šKarma Yogi›. He said, šHe lived like a Yogi and died like a Yogi.› Former Vice President of India, Justice Hidayatullah, had also applauded him for his research. His colleagues described him as ša man of sterling qualities of head and heart›; and ša dynamic and objective head of country's premier historical Institute who has left a rich legacy of his outstanding achievements in the world of historical research,› among other things.

Born on February 10, 1923, Professor Grover started his career in teaching in 1946 in Lahore and later taught at the University of Punjab and various universities in Delhi until 1974, including Delhi University, Jawahar Lal Nehru University and Jamia Milia Islamia, where he also served as head of the Department of Indian History and Culture. In 1974, he was called upon to join as Director cum Member-Secretary of the newly established Indian Council of Historical Research (ICHR), a premier historical research Institute, where he served from 1974 to 1985 as Director and was later appointed as Chairman in 1999. For his long association with ICHR, his colleague, Prof. A.R. Khan, wrote in his obituary: šOn account of his long association with the Council and the services rendered by him to it, Professor Grover became an institution by himself and he and the Council became a synonymy, as the latter came to be identified, both in India and abroad, with Professor Grover, even when he was not holding any office in the Council.

Initially having received training at Paris under the auspices of UNESCO for the promotion of history as a means of international understanding, Professor Grover wrote and published books in British history. Later, because of his deep interest in the study of original sources and his proficiency in Persian language, his research interests shifted to the medieval period of Indian history. His interest later widened to the study and research in regard to the social, cultural and economic impact of the Indian immigrants in West Asia and East European countries. As an avid researcher, Professor Grover wrote and published copiously on various aspects of the Mughal Agrarian System, Patterns of Rural Trade, The Concept of Village Community and a host of other topics. His writings, mostly published in prestigious journals, like the journals of the Delhi School of Economics and the proceedings of various conferences, became nodal points for the scholars of his generation. His published writings in

The Indian Economic and Social History Review, Proceedings of the Indian Historical Records Commission, Indian Archives, Proceedings of the Punjab History Conference, Punjab Past and Present and *The Proceedings of the Indian History Congress,* among others, brought him national and international recognition. At an early stage of Professor Grover's career, Prof. M.M. Pearson of Pennsylvania University, U.S.A., wrote about his Mughal Agrarian writings as š...an impressive start...brilliant, which makes fundamental contribution in this area.› Prof. C.A. Bailey of Cambridge University, complimented him for šcomprehensive listing of materials› and šexcellent bibliographies.›

Because of his expertise in historical manuscripts/documents and objects, Professor Grover was nominated by the Government of India for several honorary positions such as member of the Indian Historical Records Commission, member of the Historical Documents Purchase Committee of the National Archives of India, member of the Committee on Preservation and Development of Cultural Heritage of Delhi, and an expert member of the Verification Committee of National Museum, India. Professor Grover was also a member of the Publication Committee of the šComprehensive History of India›. For the Indian History Congress, he served intermittently as a Joint Secretary, a Treasurer and Sectional President (Medieval India). Professor Grover also edited the well-known Time Capsule in 1978, and advised the Government to display it in the National Museum instead of inserting it again underground. He also served on the Editorial Board constituted by the Government of India for the production of documentaries on šFreedom Struggle for India's Independence, 1984-2001.› Under this scheme, more than 75 documentaries were published by the Films Division, Ministry of Information and Broadcasting.

Professor Grover represented India at several international organizations, including UNESCO in 1951; Indian delegate to West Germany, 1957; delegate to the International Conference in History, Bucharest, 1980; delegate to the International Conference on the Bulgarian Studies, Sofia, 1986; and delegate to the World Archaeological Congress, Croatia, 1998, among others. Besides participating in numerous Indo-European cultural exchange programmes, presiding over innumerable regional/national/international seminars and conferences and contributing papers to various national/international seminars and conferences, he also lectured widely in West Germany (1957), Bulgaria (1986), Zagreb (1998), UK (1998), Holland (1998), and United States (1998 and 2000).

Professor Grover received several honours and awards for his historical research. For his writings on Georgi Dimitrov, the šRole of the Indian Immigrants in the Culture and Economy of the West Asian and East

European Countries During the Medieval Age,› and šThe Social, Religious and Agrarian Aspects in East Europe, especially Bulgaria under the Ottoman-Turkish Rule (14th-19th centuries),› he was awarded Georgi Dimitrov Gold Medal by the Peoples Republic of Bulgaria. For his work on Punjab History, Professor Grover was awarded Saropa Roll of Honour by the Punjabi University, Patiala, in 1996. A life-long scholar of medieval and Islamic India, Professor Grover again came in limelight in 2001 when (upon the demolition of Buddhist statues at Bamiyan by the Taliban government), his expert opinion was sought by the Indian media to determine whether there was any parallel between Bamiyan and Ayodhya.

As a distinguished historian and a scholar with an integrated and scientific approach to the analysis of the historical process, Professor Grover, being a liberal thinker, was a great believer in the social cohesion and national integration in India and made an immense contribution in this regard.

Preface

The present volume of the **Collected Works of Professor B.R. Grover,** pertaining to the *Zamindars* and *Jagirdars*, contributes significantly towards our understanding of the origin and interpretation of the *Zamindari* system as well as the *Jagir* system as they existed during the Mughal Age. Since the institution of *Zamindari* covered a wide range of landed interests and consisted of officials and non-officials of varying degrees and importance that was to be determined by their respective positions and ranks, it has been a difficult task for the administrators and economic historians to comprehend and interpret the origin, meaning, and usage of the term '*Zamindar*" during the Mughal rule. Professor Grover was one of the few leading historians of the Mughal period who delved into the subject matter and attempted to decipher the exact manner in which the *Zamindari* and *Jagir* systems were used in the literature of the Mughul age. Hence, the analysis presented in this volume is valuable and ought to be useful to the present-day historians in comprehending the said subject matter

The earlier literature, including the *Ain*, did not distinguish between the princely chiefs named *Zamindars* and other types of *Zamindars*. Professor Grover, through an extensive study of the original literature existing during that period on the subject matter, concluded among other things that the then-prevailing belief of three-fold divisions of the lands into *Khalsa*, *Jagirs* and *Zamindaries* had to be modified for the purposes of land administration. He iterated that a *Zamindar* owed allegiance and loyalty to the paramount power and that the criteria of allegiance lay in the acceptance of imperial limitations imposed on him and the rendering of military service to the Mughul State for which purpose he maintained his own military establishment, i.e., local militia, consisting of *sawars* and *piyada*. However, the *Zamindari* aspects could best be illustrated and understood on a regional basis, believed professor Grover. Hence, he extensively examined the position, types, rights and obligations of

Zamindars of various regions under the Mughal Empire—a description of which is contained in the present volume. This volume contains a detailed description of the Zamindars in the various regions of Gujrat, Kuch, Bihar, Assam, Bengal, Orissa, Malwa, Rajasthan, and the sub-Himalayan regions.

Another important feature of the Mughal empire that is dealt with in this volume is as to how the Mughal Emperors transferred their right to the land revenue and other taxes to their subjects of different socio-political backgrounds. The areas whose revenues were thus distributed or assigned were broadly known as *Jagirs* and the assignees were known as *Jagirdars*. According to Professor Grover, the arable and cultivated lands were broadly divided into two main categories during the Mughal age—the *khalsa* lands and the *jagir* lands. He further explained that whereas the *khalsa* lands were administered directly by the State and their revenues were basically meant for the expenditure of the Mughal Emperor, the *Jagir* lands were assigned to various categories of assignees on different terms. The present Volume of **The Collected Works** thus deals in detail with the *Jagir* system as it existed during the Mughal age and focuses on the Administration of the *Jagir*; Fiscal Rights and Obligations of *Jagirdars*; Transfer of *Jagir*; Checks on the Authority of *Jagirdars*; and the Impact of *Jagirdari* System of Mughul Administration and Peasantry.

As regards the working of the *Jagir* system, Professor Grover was of the view that any tacit recognition of the entire truthfulness of the viewpoint of the foreign travelers would reveal a great cleavage in the theory and the practice of the Mughal administration. It would mean that despite all the State directives issued to the *Jagirdars* for the welfare of the *ryots* and all regulations peraining to the assessment and collection of the revenues on the part of the assignees would merely represent the paperwork of the Mughal administration but in reality they were a complete farce. The contemporary evidence, on the contarary, proves the facts quite otherwise. However, Professor Grover stipulated that the laxity of the central government over the assignees and the local administration was quite noticeable in the last phase of Shah Jahan's reign as the agrarian condition of the country suffered tremendously by the holocaust wrought by the war of succession to the crown. He further clarified that though Aurangzeb continued to take keen personal interest, he exercised firm hold on the *khalsa* and *jagir* territories only until he shifted his seat of government to Deccan in 1681 A.D.

It is quite creditable on the part of Professor B.R. Grover to make such a serious and systematic study of the *Zamindari* system in different regions of India as well as the *Jagir* system and its workings based on contemporary and near contemporary original Persian and English documents, including literature in the regional languages found in the libraries and Archives in India and abroad. It becomes all the more noteworthy that this study was done in the 1950s when no other serious attempt in this regard had been made.

The Papers published in this Volume are being presented for the first time for the benefit of scholars of history. These papers were written during fifties of the last century. Hence, the other scholarly works published after that period have not been commented upon.

The editors of this Volume hope that this part of the **Collection of Professor B. R. Grover's Works,** as the first five volumes, will also prove valuable to the scholars interested in the economic history of the Mughal age, especially the working of *Zamindari* and *Jagir* systems, which are the most important aspects of the Mughal administration.

The editors express their sincere thanks to Shri Pradeep Mittal, Proprietor, Originals, for an excellent job in publishing this volume.

New Delhi
8th December, 2010

Miss Amrita Grover
Dr. Anju Grover Chaudhary
Dr. J.C. Dua

Introduction

It is certainly a great honour for me to write an Introduction for the second time to **The Collected Works of Professor B.R. Grover.** Professor Grover was my teacher and mentor and during my nearly four decades of academic association with him, I always found him to be a prolific and meticulous researcher. Neither subscribing to any particular school of thought nor to any ideology, he always appreciated the contributions made by his predecessors as well as contemporaries and rendered his own viewpoints based on contemporary and near contemporary original sources in Persian and other languages. He guided me to follow this approach as well.

Professor Grover invariably broke new ground by tapping original sources hitherto unknown as well as by reinterpreting the known ones. It is no wonder then that his writings have always been appreciated by scholars in India as well as abroad. His writings on *Zamindars* and *Jagirdars* are especially noteworthy as he clarified the origin, meaning and usage of the terms, among other things, that were quite confusing to the earlier historians. In fact, he was considered an expert in these areas. I am tempted to quote an incident that took place in 1969 at a Seminar where Professor Nurul Hasan Sahib read a paper on *Zamindars* and Professor Grover was one of the participants. Almost on every aspect of *Zamindars*, Professor Nurul Hasan would say, "Grover Sahib is sitting here, he knows much better tham I do." This shows his passionate interest and expertise on the subject. Professor Grover indeed was an avid researcher on various aspects of the *Zamindars*, land rights and various types of land grants and wrote copiously on the said subjects, basing his conclusions after in-depth study of original Persian and other multilingual documents.

The theme of the present Volume, the sixth in the series of **The Collected Works of Professor B.R. Grover,** is a critical appriaisal of the two most important institutions of the Mughal agrarian set-up-*Zamindars* and the *jagirdars*. Prior to his writings on the said subject, there was considerable confusion even regarding the meaning of the word '*Zamindar*'. There is no authentic proof about the origin, definition, description of the word though it is frequently mentioned in the Chronicles and the entire revenue literature from Akbar's reign to the end of the Mughal Empire. Many historians belive that the term, which literally means 'holder of land', was most probably coined in the fourteenth century. However, this term does not exist in the glossary appended to A.K.S. Lambton's *Landlord and Peasant in Persia* nor does it appear in the *Farhane-i-Rushidi*, the standard lexicon for purely Persian words. However, despite this, the term '*Zamindar*' became a standard term throughout the Mughal Empire and its local synonyms like *Satarahi, biswi* or *bisi* (in Awadh), *bhumia* (in Rajasthani) and *poligar* (in parts of South India) represented almost the same meaning.

The institution of *Zamindari* covered a wide range of landed interests, from the chiefs of the princely territories to petty intermediaries. However, even the *Ain* did not distinguish between the princely chiefs named *Zamindars* and other type of *Zamindars*. Professor Grover believed that the practice of threefold division of the lands into *Khalsa, Jagir* and *Zamindaries* had to be modified as for the purposes of land administration, even the portions of *Zamindari* territories were assigned to the State officials or to the *Zamindars* themselves in lieu of their services to the State.

The relationship between the Mughal government and the princely states has often been dismissed with the verdict that the latter were either independent or autonomous owing simply nominal allegiance by paying *peshkash* to the former. Professor Grover believed that the relations between the Mughal State as the paramount power and the Princely Chiefs could not be characterized as simply between the Paramountcy and the Indian States as in vogue during the British period of the Indian occupation. The limitations imposed by the Mughal Government upon the *Zamindaries* of the Princely Chiefs were of far more penetrating nature than visualized hitherto. Constitutionally speaking, such *Zamindaries*, with rare exceptions, could hardly be termed as States whether independent, autonomous or subordinate. After the conquest or their submission, the Princely Chiefs were initially enrolled in the circle of 'loyal *Zamindaries*' and were treated as State servants. If he was enrolled as a *Mansabdar*, he was invariably confirmed in his *watan jagir*. In lieu of his remunerations on account of *mansab* was awarded the other portions of his own *Zamindari* territory as *tankhwah jagir* and if these *jagirs* fell short of his entitlement under the *mansab* regulations, he was given an assignment from the State *jagir* lands and, at times, a portion of a territory from another *Zamindari*.

Apart from rendering of the military service to the Mughal State, a Chief *Zamindar* had to maintain law and order in his own territory. Moreover, after submission, the *Zamindari* territory was considered as part of the Mughal Empire. However, depending on its territorial extent, it was declared either as a full *sarkar* division of a neighbouring *subah* or its few *parganas* or even part of the latter.

In order to understand the true picture and characteristics of the *Zamindari* system during the Mughal Age, Professor Grover believed that it could be better understood if it was dealt on a regional basis. His theory was that it would be easy for a scholar to understand the regional variations in the working as well as in the nomenclature of the terms connected with the working of the *Zamindari* system.

It may be pointed out that as Bengal was the first Indian province to fall under the English occupation and its administration, its *Zamindari* aspects attracted the largest discussion at the hands of its early English administrators. Though in the later-Mughal period of the 18th century, the *Zamindari* system developed various new features that puzzled the English administrator-scholars about its indigenous character, in principle, the main traits of the Bengal *Zamindari* system in the 16th and, more particularly in 17th century of the Mughal Age, remained the same as in other provinces.

One of the most important features of the Mughal age was that the Mughal Emperor transferred his right to the land revenue and other taxes to certain of his subjects. The areas whose revenues were thus assigned were known as *jagirs*. *Bahar-i Azam*, the valuable Persian dictionary completed in 1739-40 (Nawal Kishor, ed., p. 283) in India offers a technical definition of the term '*jagir*' as: "*Jaigir, jagir*. A tract of land which Kings grant to *mansabdars* and (persons) of that kind, that they might take its revenue (*mahsul*) from cultivation, whatever it be."

The *jagir* lands were assigned to various categories of assignees on different terms. Assignments of various kinds, *jagir ba-mashrut* (conditional on service) and *jagir bila mashrut* (not conditional) in *inam* and *madad-i-maash* (maintenance grant) for philanthropic and charitable purposes, were made throughout the Mughal age.

The Mughal State servants could be paid their emoluments in cash (*naqdi*) or through an assignment named *tankhaw jagir*. Whether the official was to be paid in cash or in assignment, depended purely on the discretion of monarch. However, the salary of a state official, whether *naqdi* or a *jagir* was declared in cash curency of *dams*. A *Jagirdar* was entitled to the assigned land revenue and fixed share in the *sair* (miscellaneous) of the villages and *mahals* under assignments.

In his *jagir*, a *Jagirdar* exercised revenue powers for the collection of the revenue assigned to him and police and executive powers for the maintenance of the law and order in his jurisdiction. The staff thus appointed for the execution of various duties was directly responsible to the *Jagirdars*. At the same time, the *Jagirdars* were expected to increase the agricultural produce, especially of the high-grade crops and look after the welfare of the *ryots* and the *madad-i-maash* assignees in their areas. To ensure this and the application of the imperial regulations, the Mughal State provided a number of checks upon *Jagirdars*.

In the practical working of the *jagir* system during the Mughal age, there were problems faced by the assignments in the recalcitrant areas. In these areas, the fall in the revenues of *Jagirdars* as against the assessed valuation remained a constantly troublesome feature throughout the Mughal age. Though the government was committed to afford remission in the valuation of assignment and proportionate compensation, Professor Grover believed that it was rather doubtful if all the assignees were compensated on this account. Moreover, a shortage in income due to the evasion of payment of land revenue by the recalcitrant *ryots* or *Zamindars* landed many a *Mansabdar* into financial embarrassment.

Though written nearly five decades ago and despite the fact that considerable work on the Mughal land revenue had been done during the intervening period, Professor Grover's writings remain singularly distinctive and relevant even today. He will always be remembered as a distinguished and dedicated researcher in this field. I wish he had published all these writings years ago. It would have been a great inspiration for the students and researchers on the subject.

In view of the demand from scholars on the subject and the tremendous positive response from them on the release of the first five volumes in the series, the editors were encouraged to bring out further unpublished and valuable writings of Professor Grover. We are sure that like the earlier five volumes, this volume would also be apprectated and prove to beneficial to the scholars.

New Delhi **Dr. J. C. Dua**
8th December, 2010

Zamindars

1

The Zamindars

No terms in the Mughal administrative system is more important and more ambiguous and confusing than that of the Zamindar. It finds frequent mention in the *Chronicles* and the entire revenue literature from Akbar's reign to the end of the Mughal age. The origin and the complexity of its character has baffled nearly all the administrators and economic historians from the days of Warren Hastings and Sir James Grant to the recent post-independence legislation for the abolition of the *Zamindari* in the various states in India. Though it was in the last quarter of the 18th century that Grant and others analysed the institution of Mughal *Zamindari* in the territories of Bengal, Behar and Orissa, excepting a few sporadic intermittent attempts, no serious and systematic study of the *Zamindari* System in different regions of India has ever been made by any historian so far. Least of all, any analysis of the socio-economic and political significance with a bearing on the land administration has ever been attempted.

During the Mughal age, the institution of *Zamindari* covers a variety of individuals with hereditary landed interests as distinct from those of the *ryots*. It covers a wide range of landed interests, from the Chiefs of the princely territories to petty intermediaries. It comprises officials and non-officials of varying degrees and importance which is to be determined by their respective positions and ranks. Though the systems of *Zamindari* was known to the Sultanate of Delhi and the independent states of the pre-Mughal era, in some respects, it was adopted by the Mughals as such, while in others it was sufficiently replenished with new features so as to incorporate it in military and the revenue structure of the Mughal administration. Under the Mughals, it was evolved into a regular pattern of land revenue administration. The belief hitherto of the three-fold division of the lands into *Khalsa* (Crown), *Jagirs* (assignments) and *Zamindaries* (so-called princely States) has to be modified as for the purposes of land administration. Even the portions of *Zaminidari* territories were assignable to the Mughal State officials or to the Zamindars themselves in lieu of their services to the State. This is true of the Mughal administration from Akbar's reign down to the later-Mughal times.

Despite the emphasis hitherto laid on the *ryotwari* system of Akbar, it has to be conceded that the institution of *Zamindari* with its manifold aspects was a regular feature of Akbar's administration. This is well borne out by the history and detailed revenue-tables in the account of the individual *Subhas* provided in *Ain-i-Akbari* and repeated references in *Akbar Namah* and other contemporary chronicles, which when read in the light of the features of the system known from the recently discovered vast original archives of the reigns of Shah Jahan and Aurangzeb become absolutely intelligible. *Ain-i-Akbari* in its revenue-tables for most of the *Parganas* of every *Sarkar* of all the *Subahs* provided three separate columns for the Zamindars along with their castes and local militia (*Sawar* and *Piyada*) maintained by them[1]. Here, of course, *Ain* does not distinguish between the princely chiefs named Zamindars and other type of Zamindars. But the fact that the contingent of local militia maintained by the latter varies from *Paragana* to *Paragana* is quite suggestive. At times, the number of the contingent in a *Paragana* is so small[2] that it would be ridiculous to associate it essentially with the princely Zamindars. The picture about certain categories of Zamindars becomes clearer in Jahangir's reign as known from *Baharistan-i-Chaibi* of Mirza Nathan. For the reigns of Shah Jahan and Aurangzeb, now there is no dearth of original archives which clearly illustrate the respective position of every type of Zamindar. Thus, the Zamindars may be classified into various categories.

Though Babur in his description of Hindustan usually uses the term of Zamindar in a very wide sense so as to call the rulers of seven independent kingdoms, Delhi, Jaunpur, Gujrat, Bahmani (Deccan), Malwa, Bengal, Vijyanagar (Deccan) and Mewar as the big Zamindars of India,[3] the hereditary ruling chiefs entitled *Rajas*, *Maharanas*, *Ranas*, *Rawats*, *Raos* and *Rais* were essentially known as Zamindars and their domains as *Zamindaries*.[4] Technically, such Zamindars with a territorial jurisdiction of at least a *Pargana* or more were designated as *Zamindars-i Umda* (High dignitary or Chief Zamindars) as distinguished from smaller Zamindars known simply as Zamindars with a *Zamindari* of a few villages or at times even a single village in a *Paragana*.[5]

As regards the relationship between the Mughal Government and such Zamindars (Princely Chiefs), it has often been dismissed with the verdict that the latter were either independent or autonomous owing simply nominal allegiance paying *Peshkash* (fixed revenues tribute) to the former.[6] Such an analysis is based on a fallaçious political concept and belies the real character of the Mughal polity and agrarian set up. The relations between the Imperialist Mughal State as the Paramount Power and the Princely Chiefs cannot be characterized as simply between the Paramountcy and the Indian States as in vogue during the British period of the Indian occupation.[7] The limitations imposed by the Mughal Government upon the Zamindaries of the Princely Chiefs were of far more penetrating nature than visualised hitherto and constitutionally speaking, with rare exceptions, such *Zamindaries* can hardly be termed as States whether independent, autonomous or subordinate.

The process of Mughal conquest of the Indian sub-continent and the nature of its occupation was based on five-fold concept which determined its relations with the Zamindars. Firstly, the conquest of a territory of a pre-Mughal sultanate or a Chieftainship would result in an outright annexation to the Mughal territories, further divided into the *Khalsa* and the *Jagirs* but administered directly by the State servants. Secondly, within these pre-Mughal States, there had been *Zamindaries* under the princely Chiefs who had either paid nominal allegiance or *Peshkash* (tribute) to the Sultans or as distinct from these, there were still Chieftainships which had retained their independence. After the conquest or their submission to the Mughal Government, based on a treaty, their rights and obligations were confirmed through a Royal *Farman*. They were all enrolled in the circle of 'loyal Zamindars' and were treated as State servants.[8] As such, though they were confirmed in their *Zamindari* rights and privileges, with extremely rare exceptions, they were essentially obliged to render military service to the Paramount Power. Territorially, each *Zamindari* consisted of two portions, namely hereditary *Watan Jagir* (patrimony) and the other territory under its jurisdiction. At times, after submission, a *Zamindari* was shelved of certain portions of its territory which were incorporated in the *Khalsa* lands. Many of these Zamindars were confirmed in their entire *Zamindaries* comprising the *Watan Jagir* and the other territory being treated as either *Inam* (gift) *Jagir* or as *Tankhwah Jagir* (for remunerations) in lieu of the military service. But they had to pay fixed *Peshkash* (tribute) per annum to the Mughal Government. Thirdly, at times, even though nominally vested with the entire *Zamindari*, they were entitled to the revenues of the *Watan Jagir* and some other portion of the *Zamindari*, assigned in proportion to the extent, revenues and the military contingent maintained by them. They acted as tax-gatherers for the rest of the territory and were required to pay the land revenue as fixed lump sum (*peshkash*) in installments. Fourthly, a majority of the Zamindars, though nominally retained the entire *Zamindari*, had a claim for the revenues only upon the *Watan Jagir* whereas the other territory was assigned in *tankhawah Jagir* to other *Jagirdars* who were the official *mansabdars* of the Mughal States. Fifthly, if a Zamindar himself was enrolled as a *Mansabdar*, he was invariably confirmed in his *Watan Jagir* and in lieu of his remunerations on account of *mansab*, was awarded the other portions of his own *Zamindari* territory as '*Tankhwah' Jagir* and if these *Jagirs* fell short of his entitlement under the *mansab* regulations, he was given an assignment from the State *Jagir* lands and at times a portions of a territory from another *Zamindari*. In case of a fresh succession to the *Zamindari*, excepting the *Watan-Jagir*, all other *Jagir* lands of the deceased lapsed to the Mughal State, though invariably, the succeeding Zamindar was awarded a *mansab* in lieu of which he was restored the other territory of his own *Zamindari* as *Jagir* land. How a *Zamindari* was placed in a particular category depended upon numerous factors, the political expendiency, the family tradition of the ruling Chief, the nature of submission, whether voluntary or after resistance, and the geographical and strategic situation of the *Zamindari* with a possibility of future resistance. The nature of the category of a *Zamindari* was also alterable. A loyal Zamindar owing regular allegiance and military service could improve his position whereas a recalcitrant Zamindar could be degraded and at times after appointment he would endanger the entire Zamindari which would be attached to *Khalsa* land.

As regards obligations, a Zamindar owed allegiance and loyalty to the Paramount Power, the criteria of allegiance lay in the acceptance of Imperial limitations imposed on him and the rendering of the military establishment i.e. local militias, consisting of cavalry (*Sawars*) and infantry (*Piyada*).[9] He could be called upon to fight against any recalcitrant Zamindar who either rebelled or defied the Imperial expansion. A Zamindar could belong to either of the cadres, the Provincial Service or Imperial Service.[10] In the former case, he had to fight for the Mughal Government within the territorial limits or proximity of his own Province. In the latter case, he was enrolled as a regular *mansabdar* in the Imperial Army and could be called to serve anywhere in the Indian subcontinent[11] and barring very few exceptions,[12] even abroad on the North-Western Frontier and in Central Asia. A regional study of the pre-Mughal age shows that where Zamindars owed military allegiance to the Sultanate, because of the limited territorial extent of the latter, the military service on the part of the Zamindars too was inevitably circumscribed to the regional limits. In contrast to it, despite its territorial expansion, the Mughal Empire accepted the prevailing custom as it suited its local needs both for defence and expansion.[13] At the same time, the vastness of the Empire and political expediency led Akbar to reorienate the Imperial policy towards the

Zamindars. Many of the loyal Zamindars were enrolled as regular *mansabdars* in the Imperial Army, who also constituted henceforth a notable part of the Mughal nobility. This policy was continued till the end of the Mughal age.

Apart from the military service, a Chief Zamindar had to maintain law and order in his own territory.[14] He could not wage war against any other *Jagirdar* or Zamindar and in case of any territorial dispute, it had to be essentially referred to the Mughal Court.[15] Even though hereditary in character, the succession to the "*Gaddi*" of a Chief *Zamindari* was subject to confirmation by the Mughal Court which had the prerogative to regulate it.[16] As for his priviledges, apart from the *Jagir* assignments, he was entitled to hold his own court and exercised judicial, executive and revenue powers in his territory.[17] He could make further assignments both for military and charitable purposes.[18] For his relations with the Mughal Government, a chief Zamindar dealt directly with the Central Government and was represented at the Mughal Court by his *Vakil* (Agent).[19] But for all matters of *Jagir* assignments, he had equally to deal with the *Subahdar* and *Diwan-i-Subah*.[20] An ordinary Zamindar had to deal with the Provincial authorities though for any matter he had the right to make direct representation to the Central Court.[21] A Zamindar paying *Peshkash* fell under the jurisdiction of the Provincial authorities and the *Faujdar* of the division dealing with his *Zamindari*.[22] A petty Zamindar was exempted from military service though he maintained a small local militia for the preservation of law and order and the collection of land revenue. He was assigned a small *Jagir* in lieu of his services.

As regards land revenue administration, the *Zamindari* lands may be divided into two catagories, *Ghair Amli* and *Amli*.[23] The latter comprised land which was brought under Mughal methods of survey, measurement, prepararation of villagewise record-of-rights and assessment thereof. Contrary to this, the *Ghair Amli* land was not subject to Mughal methods of land administration. In some cases, the entire *Zamindari* was declared as *Ghair Amli*, in others as *Amli*, while in still other cases, if the territory other than the *Jagirs* of the Zamindar was assignable to any other *Jagirdar*, it was declared *Amli* whereas the Zamindar's own *Jagirs* continued to be treated as *Ghair Amli*. In his *Ghair-amli* portions of the *Zamindari*, the Zamindar pursued indigenous methods of assessment and fixed incidence of land revenue based on traditional notions. It seems that in most of the regions in India, the burden of the land revenue upon the cultivators in the *Zamindari* lands was higher in comparision to the land revenue fixed in the territories administered directly by the Mughal Government.[24] The *amli* portions in a *Zamindari*, if any, were subject to Mughal methods of survey and assessment. *Ain* provides measurement figures of the Imperial *Paraganas* and for such of the *Zamindari* areas decleared *Amli*, while for the *Ghair Amli* areas, for want of recorded date, the measurement column is left blank. The Zamindar had his own machinery and staff for the collection of the revenue through the agency of the village officials.

After submission, the *Zamindari* territory was considered as a part of the Mughal Empire and depending on its territorial extent was declared either as a full *Sarkar* division of a neighbouring *subah* or its few *Parganas* or even as a part of the latter. Thus, along with the directly administered Imperial territories, all *Zamindaries* conquered in Akbar's reign find a parallel description in the narrative account and the revenue tables provided in the Ain-i-Akbari.[25] Of course, in the *Pargana*-wise revenue figures, Ain does not make any distinction between the Imperial territories and the Zamindar. But all the same, it gives consolidated figures of the local militia for each *Subah* and *Sarkar* and *Paragana*-wise statement without discrimination between the different categories of the Zamindaries. It also provides measurement figures for the *Amli* areas. That such a practice of incorporation of the freshly acquired Zamindaries continued even after Akbar's reign is well authenticated by the contemporary sources.

The Zamindari aspects known hitherto can be best illustrated on regional basis, viz. in Gujrat, Rajasthan, Bengal, Orissa, Assam and the sub-Himalayan ranges.

2

Zamindars of Gujrat

The detailed description of the *Zamindaries* in Gujrat, available both in *Mirat-i-Ahamdi* and *Ain,* entitles them to priority in analysis. *Mirat* distinguishes between the two main classes of *Zamindaries, Zamindaran-i Umda* (high dignitary) and the ordinary Zamindars[26] and both are further divided into two categories each. Of the Chief Zamindars, some had to pay fixed *Peshkash* (tribute) while others were exempted from it. *Mirat* enumerates six *Chief Zamindars*, viz of *Dungarpur, Banswarah, Sirohi, Cutch, Sunth and Ramnagar who paid annual Peshkash.*[27] Historically, all the six *Zamindaries* had formed part of the Sultanate of Gujrat, but after the Mughal conquest were parceled out in the two *Subhas* of Gujrat, and Ajmer. Though in the historical and geographical narrative, *Ain* treats *Banswarah, Dungarpur and Sirohi in the Subah of Gujrat,* technically it counts them in *Sarkar Sirohi of Subah Ajmer.*[28] And, as such, shall be dealt with amongst the Rajasthan Chief. Under Akbar, the Zamindars of *Cutch, Sunth and Ramnagar* accepted the Mughal paramountcy and were allowed to remain in their respective possessions on two-fold conditions of payment of fixed *Peshkash* per annum both in cash and presents, and rendering of the *military service.* The *Zamindari* was regarded as a conditional *Jagir* contingent on military service.[29] The armed contingent of *Sawars* (Cavalry) and *Piyada* (footmen) to be supplied by them was fixed with due regard to the extent and revenues of their respective *Jagirs* and the armed forces maintained by them. [30] *This was reviewed from time to time.*[31]

Ain mentions the Zamindar of *Cutch* belonging to Yadu race and *Jareju* tribe, maintaining a military force of 10,000 cavalry and 50,000 infantry.[32] The *Zamindari* was accredited to *Sarkar* Surat.[33] In return for the services rendered by *Bahara Khankar the Zamindar* to *Khan-i- Azam* Mirza Aziz Kokaltash in getting Sultan Muzaffar Khan of Gujrat captured, the Zamindar was exempted from military services for some time but early in

Jahagir's reign was required to supply 2,000 cavalry. Apart from the confirmation of his Pre Mughal *Zamindari* of 1449 villages, in lieu of the above mentioned services, he was assigned the *Pargana* of Morvi and the villages of Keri, Sathalpur, Kanikot in *Pargana* Murdawara (*Sarkar* Sorath) and *Pargana* Rajbar (In Thatta, *Subah* Multan).[34] The entire *Zamindari* was *Ghair-amli*. The Chief of Cutch throughout remained a loyal Zamindar and paid annual *Peshkash*.[35] The Zamindar of *Ramnagar*, accredited to *Sarkar* Surat, was confirmed in his territory by Todar Mal of Akbar's reign on the condition of supplying 1,000 cavalry and a fixed tribute. The Zamindar of *Sunth* was recognized on the condition of military service and a fixed tribute of Rs. 15,000 per annum.[36] The Zamindars of *Nawanagar* and *Baglana* accepted the Mughal authority and undertook to pay *Peshkash* and render military service but both of them were always recalcitrant and consequently their *Zamindaries* were annexed to the Mughal Empire. The Zamindar of *Nawanagar*, named as *Jam*, maintained a force of 7000 cavalry and 8,000 infantry[37] and owed a contigent of 4,000 *Sawars* to the Pre-Mughal Gujrat Sultanate.[38] Though status-quo was maintained in respect of his *Zamindari*, he was required to pay *Peshkash* and render military service with a contingent of 2,000 *Sawars*, accredited to *Sarkar* Surat.[39] Since he was often recalcitrant in the discharge of these obligations, his *Zamindari* was incorporated in the Mughal Empire in Aurangzeb's reign (1074 A.H.) and was declared as a separate *Sarkar* named Islam Nagar. Through the interventation of Maharaja Jaswant Singhji, *Nazim* of the Province, the recognition of the *Jam* and his sons was retained but they were left only with a small *Jagir* of nine divisions from *Pargana Khambalia*.[40] The Zamindar of *Baglana*, popularly known as the Chief of Salher and Mulhar commanded a force of 3,000 cavalry and 10,000 infantry[41] and had owed a contingent of 3,000 cavalry to the Sultanate of Gujrat.[42] Under Akbar, he was confirmed in his *Zamindari* on the same military condition and payment of *Peshkash* accredited to Sarkar Surat. As the Chief was often recalcitrant, in Shahjahan's reign, the territory of Baglana was annexed to the Mughal Empire in 1637 A.D. by Prince Aurangzeb.[44] It was incorporated in the *Khalsa* land and was declared a *Sarkar* division of *Subah Khandesh*.[45] The Chief Zamindar of *Junagarh*, because of *recalcitrance*, had been forced to submission in Akbar's reign by Khan-i-Azam Mirza Aziz Kokatashin in 1000 A.H. and his *Zamindari* was incorporated in the Mughal Empire as one of the *Paraganas* of new Sorath.

Apart from the Chief Zamindars, there were other hereditary Zamindars with comparative limited territorial jurisdiction who were all confirmed by the Mughal Government. Such a *Zamindari* comprised either a full

Paragana or a few villages of a *Paragana.* Various families viz. *Girasia,* Rajputs, Kolis, Kathis, Jats, Jhadejas, Bakhirs, Koraishis, Rathors, Ahirs, Makwanas and Muslims with such ancient *Zamindaries* maintained status-quo in the Mughal age.[47] These *Zamindaries* were established in ancient chaotic times but during the Muslim sultanate of Gujrat, they all undertook to serve the State and pay the land revenue. They were given one-fourth of the *Zamindari* territory known as *Banth* as *Watan*-villages (Patrimonions *Jagirs*) for their maintenance while revenues of the three-fourth of the territory named *Talpad* were to be deposited in the State treasury.[48] Excepting the revenues of the *Watan Jagir,* the Zamindar was not entitled to the revenue of the other territory of his *Zamindari*, which if not assigned to any other *Jagirdar*, had to be paid in instalments as *Peshkash* to the Mughal State.[49] An Akbar's *Farman* dated A.H. 999/1590 A.D. confirms the status-quo and directs the *Diwan* or *Subah* Gujrat to essentially afford *Banth* (one-fourth of the land) to the *Kolis* etc. (Zamindars) and to exempt it from the payment of land revenue. It also enjoins him to take sureties for the proper conduct of the Zamindars.[50]

In respect of their obligations in lieu of the *Banth* possession (*Watan Jagir*), such Zamindars fall into two divisions, those holding a full *Pargana* had to render military service with a full *Pargana* had to render military service with a fixed contingent while the holders of only a *Taraf* (division of a Pargana) of a few villages in a *Pargana* paid *Salami* i.e. nominal quit-rent for allegiance.[51] Thus, of those owing military service, accredited to *Sarkar Surat*, the Zamindars of Idar, Rajpipla, Ali and Mohan, though of their own owing much larger forces, supplied cavalry contingent of 500, 2,000, 500 and 300 respectively.[52] The Zamindar of Idar, Punjah Rathor, in lieu of the *Watan Jagir* had owed a contingent of 2,000 *sawars* to the Sultanate of Gujrat and was exempted from the payment of *Peshkash.* He also held 100 villages in *Inam-Jagir* in *Pargana* Mangrej.[53] His son, Narain Das, after defeat at the hands of the Mughal forces, was reduced to submission and confirmed in his *Zamindari.*[54] Due to the oft-repeated recalcitrance of the Chiefs, *Zamindari* was twice brought under direct Mughal rule, in 986 A.H. with Wazir Khan as administrator during the Governorship of Shahhuddin Ahmed Khan and in 1656 A.D. with Sayyed *Hato* during the Governership of Prince Murad Baksh.[55] But in Aurangzeb's reign, it was finally annexed to the Mughal territories in 1083 A.H. and Mohammad Bahlol was appointed as the *Faujdar* of Idar.[56] The Zamindar of Rajpipla (*Sarkar* Nandod) was confirmed in Akbar's reign during the Governorship of Shahbuddin Ahemad Khan.[57] Similarly, the Zamindars of *Mohan* and *Ali* (*Sarkar* Champaner) were confirmed in Akbar's reign.[58] There are other full *Pargana Zamindaries* owing similar military obligations but it is difficult to work out the entire situation as *Ain* in its narrative explains the *Zamindaries* on tribal basis in terms of two general geographical divisions,[59] irrespective of their detailed classification.

Apart from the Chief *Zamindaries*, *Mirat* affords mostly combined information in respect of *Zamindaries* with a full *Pargana* or a division thereof.[60] Of course, the fixation of contingent was done in proportion to the extent and the revenues of their respective *Jagirs*.[61] The petty *Zamindaries* comprising only a few villages can be traced in practically most of the *Parganas* of all the *Sarkars*.[62] Though *Ain*, as for all Provinces, indicates the prevalence of such *Zamindaries* in most of the *Parganas* with the names of the tribes and armed contingent maintained by them, it does not give villagewise details of each *Pargana*. But *Mirat* affords various examples. In *Pargana* Azamabad (*Sarkar* Ahmadabad), the Zamindars of Attarsumba, Mandva, Haldarwas, Ghorasar used to pay fixed annual *Peshkash* during the Sultanate period and were confirmed as such in the Mughal age.[63] The *Parganas* of Palanpur and Kheralu (*Sarkar* Pattan) have 179 and 114 villages out of which 29 and 51 belonged to the Zamindars respectively.[64] At times, one *Pargana* though entirely *Zamindari*, is divided amongst various Zamindars. For example, Pargana Utleshwar (*Sarkar* Broach) forms one division under the local Zamindars.[65] *Ain's* enumeration of more than one caste or tribe for the Zamindars is equally suggestive of multiple *Zamindaries* in a *Pargana*. The fixation of the quit-rent (*Salami*) of each petty *Zamindari* was always done in proportion to the number of houses settled and the cultivable land in the personal possession of a Zamindar.[66] All these Zamindars had to look after the preservation of law and order in their territories.[67]

As regards land revenue administration, many of such *Zamindaries* were *Ghair amli* while others were *amli*. For example, for the full *Pargana Zamindaries* of Mohan (*Sarkar* Champner) Utleshwar (*Sarkar* Broach), Denhor (*Sarkar* Sorath), six unnamed Parganas in *Sarkar* Godhra, though shown with revenue figures are specifically mentioned as *Ghair amli*.[68] Some of the *Parganas* were *amli*. When the Zamindar of Rajpipla accepted Mughal authority, *Desais, Qazis* and Reporters were appointed by the Mughal Government in these territories. As one of the *Desais* was killed, the *Nazim* invaded the territory and imposed upon the Zamindar Rs.1,00,000 as tribute as a penalty.[69] In all such *amli* territories, *Desais* were appointed by Government for the purposes of survey and assessment.[70] Of the petty *Zamindaries*, though a few of them remained *Ghair amli*, invariably, they were declared *amli*. On the contrary, for various quit-rent paying *Zamindari Parganas, Mirut* also associates *Desais* (revenue officials) with them, which, were essentially *amli*. For example , the tables for the *Parganas* of

Bahiel, Birpur, Paplod, Parantijx, Modasa (*Sarkar* Ahmadabad), Pattan, Bijapur, Disah (*Sarkar* Pattan, north), Baroda, Bahadurpur, Sinor (*Sarkar* Baroda south), Charasi (*Sarkar* Champaner) quote the amount of quit-rent paid by the Zamindars and the remunerations of the *Desais.*[72] That they were essentially *amli* areas is further confirmed by the fact that for each of the latter *Parganas, Ain* provides measurement figures in terms of *bighas* and for many of these even *Suyurghal* (*madad-i maash* assignments) amounts are mentioned.[73] As to the procedure of the revenue collection in the *Talpad* area (the territory besides the *Watan Jagir*) the collection was left to the Zamindar himself who would pay it to the State as *Peshkash.* But usually, it was assigned in *Jagir* to State officials.[74] In case of a habitual recalcitrant (*Zur Talab*) Zamindar, the assignment was made to a powerful *Faujdar* who could enforce his authority for the realization of the revenues.[75] Of the petty *Zamindaries*, their *Talpad* areas could be declared either a part of the *Khalsa* or *Jagir* of any state official. This is confirmed by Akbar's *Farman* which enjoins the *Khalsa* officials and the *Jagirdars* not to coerce the Zamindars and to essentially afford them the revenues of their *Banth* areas.[76] Ordinarily, for forcing the Zamindar for the payment of the land revenue for the *Talpad* area or if assigned, for helloing the assignees, Such Zamindaries were a accredited to a *Faujdari* division and even *Faujdari thanas* were set up within the *Zamindaries.*[77] Many of the sea ports on the Western Coast, even though incorporated in the *Khalsa* administration, were technically treated as petty *Zamindaries.* The Zamindar of a Port was entitled to one-fourth of the income in lieu of service for the safety of the Port.[78]

Footnotes of Chapter 1 & 2

1. All the copies of the *Ain* Mss that I have consulted (Ms. Hamilton I, Berlin, Br. M. Add 7652 and Add 6552, Suppl. Pers. 277 B.N. Paris, Ms. Or. Sprenger 229 Berlin, Kapurthala Ms. State Archives Patiala; Nos. 2011 & 935 Tonk Collection N.A.I.) put the arrangement for the description of the data in the *Parganas* of the *Sarkars* in the following order:

(i) *Parganat* (*Parganas* to be named) (ii) *Qulah* (Forts) (iii) *Arazi* (Measured land in terms of *Bighas*)(iv) *Naqdi* (Revenue in dams) (v) *Suyurghal* (*Madad-i-Maash* assignments in dams) (vi) Zamindars (vii) *Sawar* (Cavalry) (viii) *Piyada* (infantry). Against column with, the castes and tribal names of the Zamindars and the dominant population in the *Pargana* areas are entered. Columns vii and viii show the cavalry and the infantry maintained by the Zamindars. Jarrett's *Ain* puts these headings in a different order (i) *Parganas*, its names and also mentioning a fort, if any. (ii) *Bighas* and *Biswas* (iii) Revenue (D) (iv) *Suryurghal* (D) (v) Cavalry (vi) Infantry (vii) Castes. Jarrett's substitutions of *Bighas* and *Biswas* for "*Arazi*" and "*Castes*" for Zamindar is not correct. Dr. Irfan Habib's criticism of Jarrett (vide '*The Zamindars in the Ain*', I.H.C. Proceedings 1958, Pp. 320-23) is justified. Though Dr. Habib correctly suggests the existence of a class of Zamindars other than the Princely Chiefs, he has not analysed the nature of either of these.

2. *Ain*, J. tr. Pp. 202-3, N.A.I. no 2011. Tonk collection fol. 164a. For example, for some of the *Parganas* in Sarkar Alwar, *Subah* Agra, the table follows:

Pargana	*Zamindars with Castes*	*Cavalry*	*Infantry*
Mandauar	*Chauhan*	4	20
Panain	*Khan Zadah* and *Meo*	5	50
Bhiwai	Various	5	50
Basana	Do	5	50

3. *Tuzuk-I Babri*, B.N. Paris, fol.

4. *Ibid*; also see discussion on 'Zamindars in Rajasthan'.

5. *Mirat*. I. pp. 173-74; B.G. tr. I.P. 319.

6. Dr. P. Saran, 'The Provincial Government', pp. 111-116; Sharma. S.R. 'Mughal Government and Administration', pp. 223-28.

7. *Ibid*. The relations between the East India Company and later on the Crown and the Indian States were based on quite a different concept. Dr. Saran's analogy in this respect is vague and incorrect.

8. B.G. tr. II. P 517.

9. *Ain* vide, ref. no.1. Also see discussion on 'Zamindars in Gujrat, Rajasthan and Bengal'.

10. B.G. tr. I., p. 431.

11. See, for example, 'Zamindars in Rajasthan'.

12. See treaty between Jahangir and Rana Karan Singh of Mewar vide reference no in 'Zamindars in Rajasthan'.

13. B.G. tr. II, pp. 503-4, 517-22, 566-70.

14. *Mirat* I., p. 174.

15. Vir Vinod, pp. 730-47. Quotes original correspondence in Persian and Rajasthani between Jamadtul mulk Asad Khan Aurangzeb's minister and Maharana Amar Singh II of Mewar through his Vakil Kishav Rai about the disputed *Parganas* of PurMandal, Badnor and Mandalgarh, which were consequently restored to Karan Singh and Jhajjar Singh, the *Jagirdars*. Also, Asad Khan's Letter to Rawal Ajab Singh to restore 27 border villages of Bhilwara etc. in *Zillah* Dhangal in Udaipur's Zamindari and not to interfere in the latter's territory.

16. See discussion in 'Zamindars in Rajasthan'.

17. Travernier, pp. 57-58.

18. Of the *Paṭta* grants of Mewar at Chief Commissioner's Office Udaipur, a Copper-Plate Inscription no 214 dated 15th bright half of *Kartik*, V.S. 1631/ 29th October, 1574 A.D. notes in Mewari text the land grant by Rana Pratap to Joshi Puno for being posted as the head of the cavalry at Haldighati. Another Copper-plate Inscription, Mewari text no. 94. *Jagir*, S. 91 C.O. Udaipur, dated 14th bright half of *Vaishakh*, V.S. 1724/27th April, 1667 A.D. records the grant to *Piths*, the leader of Bhils. Also Tod's 'Rajasthan', pp. 163-64. Appendix no V. quotes a *Patta* grant (dated Pos. V.S. 1798) of *Pargana* Bhynsrore by Maharaja Jagat Singh to Rawat Lal Singh Kesurisingote Commander.

19. R.A.J., *Vakil* reports. See Bibligraphy; *Vir Vinod*. pp. 735-36; 740-51. Quotes original correspondence between Maha Rana Amar Singh II of Mewar through his *Vakils* with the Central Government and the Governor of Malwa regarding the disputed *Parganas*.

20. *Vir Vinod*, pp. 734-35.

21. *Mirat*. I., p. 173; *Vir VInod*, p. 735.

22. *Ibid*. p. 189; *Mirat*. Suppl. pp. 190, 205-6, 219; B.G. tr. I., p. 213 mentions that even *Shiqdars* could exact tribute from the Zamindars.

23. *Amal* means pertaining to land revenue. But when associated with an area termed *Amali*, it acquires a technical sense denoting a land wherein State demand (*Jama*) has been fixed after regular survey, assessment and villagewise record of rights. D.B.S.D. fols. 145a-219b gives villagewise record of assessed 'Jama' for the *Amli Parganas* or *Mahals* whereas for the *Ghair amli* (Not *Amli*) only a consolidated amount for the entire *Mahal* or *Zamindari* is given. For the *Amli Mahals* (fols 218a-219b) it clearly mentions that their '*Jama*' is based on survey and assessment (*Muwafiq-i Tashkhish*) while for the *Ghair Amli* it states on the testimony of *Qanungos* that villagewise assessment

records are not available (*Dehi Bedehi narisida*) Wilson's definition of *Amali* (vide Glossary p. 21) as, "Payment of revenue by a division of the crop or in kind" is too rigid and incorrect. *Mahazar-i Shahjahani,* pp 19, 51; 101-3, associates the term *Amal* with different methods of land revenue viz. *Amal-i Ghallabakshi* (here in Wilsonian sense), *Amal-i Zabti, Amali Ijara.* At the same time, the term when associated with an individual official would mean an act of revenue administration viz. dar *Amal-i Karori, dar Amal-i Jagirdar* (*Ibid.* pp. 89-170 R.A.J. uncatalogued *Pargana* documents). Though it is possible that the term *Amali* may have acquired a customary meaning in a particular region at the time of Wilson's codification, it is not borne by the Mughal archival revenue documents. Dr. Yusuf Hussain's concurrence with Wilson vide 'Selected *Waqai* of the Deccan', p. 142, is not correct for the analysis of the document (vide P. 125 Pers. text) under annotation.

24. B.G. tr. I. pp. 369-371.

25. *Ain* J. tr. II. Vide Account of the Twelve *Subahs,* pp. 129-370.

26. *Mirat.* I., pp. 173-75.

27. *Mirat.* Suppl., pp. 224-228.

28. *Ain.* J. tr. II. p. 281.

29. *Mirat.* I. p. 174.

30. *Ibid.*

31. *Ibid.*, p. 189. In Jahangir's reign, during the Governorship of Khan-i Azam Aziz Kokaltash, contingents were fixed for the *Zamindaries*, accredited to *Sarkar Surat*, for a term of four years.

32. *Ain*, J. tr. II., pp. 255-56.

33. *Mirat.*, I., p. 189.

34. *Ibid*, p. 22, Suppl. pp. 226-27.

35. *Ibid.* Suppl. The Zamindar also made presents to Prince Khurram at the latter's visit (*Ibid.*, p. 194) and later in Aurangzeb's reign had to pay *Peshkash* of 3 lacs *Mahmudis* as penalty for having kept in custody the goods and jewelry of Prince Dara Shikho after the War of Succession.

36. *Ibid.*, Suppl. p. 228. During the Gujrat Sultanate period, Harbans Zamindars of Sunth had also a *Mahal* in Sarkar Ghodara on the condition of military service but exempted from the payment of its revenue (*Ibid.*, I., p. 21).

37. *Ain*, J. tr. II. p. 256.

38. *Mirat,* I., p. 22.

39. *Ibid.*, pp. 189, 193. During Jahagir's reign, a levy of military contigent was fixed at 2,000 Sawars. Later on, during Azim Khan's Governorship (Shahjahan's reign) on account of recalcitrance Nawanagar was invaded and the Zamindar was forced to pay *Peshkash* and surrender his right of minting coinage. (*Ibid.*, pp. 213-216).

40. *Ibid.*, pp. 254-55, *Ibid.*, Suppl. pp. 219-20.

41. *Ain,* J. tr. II. p. 257, *Mirat,* I., p. 189.

42. *Mirat*, I., p. 21.

43. *Ibid.*, p. 189.

44. B.N. Lahori, Bib. Ind. Pers. text. II., pp. 106-9; *Bombay Gazetteer*, Nasik Park II, pp. 403-4; Sarkar's *Aurangzeb,* I., pp. 50-53.

45. *Roznamcha-i Waqainawis-i Baglana,* dated 18th *Rabi* II, A.H. 1072/11th Dec., 1661 A.D. C.R.O. Hyderabad; also 'Selected *Waqai*', *Roznamchas,* Pers. text. p. 140; also my article on '*Diwan -i Sarkar*', vide I.H.R.C. 1962.

46. *Mirat,* I., pp. 177-79.

47. *Ibid.*, pp. 171-73 vide *Akbar's Farman*; *Ibid.*, p. 225.

48. *Ibid.*, pp. 21, 173-74, *Ibid.*, Suppl. pp. 228-29.

49. *Ibid.*, Suppl. pp. 228-239. The term *'Peshkash'* is used in general. It stands for the fixed annual tribute, penalty imposed, and even for land revenue in the *Zamindari* areas occurring to the Mughal State. It has to be interpreted according to the context. The revenues realised from the *Zamindaries* as *Peshkash* were regularly assessed.

50. *Ibid.*, pp. 172-73.

51. *Ibid.*, Suppl., p. 229.

52. *Ibid.*, I., p. 189.

53. *Ibid.*, pp. 18, 22.

54. *Ibid.*, p. 134. *Ain,* J. tr., II., p. 248 states, "The Chief of Idar is a Zamindar named Narian Dass...... He is regarded as the head of the Rathor trible and has a following of 500 horse and 10,000 foot."

55. *Ibid.*, p. 138, *Vir Vinod*, p. 996.

56. *Ibid.*, p. 294.

57. *Ibid.*, p. 140, *Mirat Suppl.*, p. 233 states that in the reign of the Sultans of Gujrat, the Zamindar of Rajpipla had one-fourth in the *Pargana* of Nandod with 16 *Parganas* near Nandurbar. Under Akbar, he was confirmed with the status quo by Raja Todar Mal on the condition of serving with 1,000 *Sawars*.

58. *Ibid.*, Suppl. p . 233. Mohan paid 52,000 *mahmudis* and Ali 1,00,000 *mahmudis* respectively as *Peshkash* in Aurangzeb's reign in lieu of the revenues of the other territory than the *Watan-Jagir*.

59. *Ain.* J., tr. II., pp. 246-257.

60. *Mirat,* Suppl., pp. 228-239. Apart from it, seven *Ghair amli Parganas* in *Sarkar* Godhra (p. 211) and 15 *Ghair amli Parganas* in *Sarkar* Sorath (p. 219) are stated to be with Zamindars.

61. *Ibid.*, I., p. 174.

62. *Ibid.*, Suppl. pp. 228-39 quotes 117 *Parganas* or their divisions (*Tarafs*) wherein Zamindars paid *Peshkash* in lieu of the revenues of their respective territories other than the *Watan-Jagirs*.

63. *Ibid.*, p. 190.

64. *Ibid.*, pp. 200-1, 205.

65. *Ibid.*, p. 205.

66. *Ibid.*, p. 229.

67. *Ibid.*, I., p. 174.

68. *Ibid.*, pp. 209, 205, 216, 211 respectively.

69. *Ibid.*, p. 233.

70. *Ibid.*, pp. 236-39 *Mirat* quotes 63 other *Zamindari Parganas* wherein *Desais* were appointed. It seems that the *Zamindari Pargana* of Idar was *Ghair amli* (vide *Ain*, J. tr. II., p. 258, it has no measurement figures) and the position narrated for it in *Mirat Suppl.*, pp. 190, 236 applies to its post-annexation period.

71. *Ibid.*, p. 203.

72. *Ibid.*, pp. 236-239.

73. *Ain,* J., tr., pp. 258-61.

74. *Ain,* J., tr. II., pp. 254-55 comments, "In the seventh district are the *Baghelas*. It furnishes 200 horse and the same number of foot. The *Kathis* are numerous in this tract; they are of *Ahir* caste...... The military force is 6,000 cavalry and 6,000 infantry.......When any *Jagirdar* comes amongst them, they make it a condition that there shall be no account taken of the inconvenience of any of their people." Also, Suppl. p. 205-6, for example, the *Zamindari Parganas* of Atleshwar and Chermandvi (*Sarkar* Broach) were usually assigned to the *mutsaddi* of *Sarkar* Surat. The *Zamindari Pargana* of Halvad (*Sarkar Sorath*, p. 219) was assigned with *thanas* established therein. In contrast to this, certain *Parganas* were never assigned. For instance, *Pargana* Tarkeshwar (*Sarkar Broach* p. 206) being mountainous was neither assigned to any *Jagirdar* nor connected with any *Faujdari*.

75. *Ibid.*

76. *Ibid.*, I., p. 173.

77. *Ibid.* For example, the *Zamindaries* of Attarsumba, Mandva, Haldawaras, Ghorasar (p. 190) were attached with the *Faujdari* of *Pargana* Azamabad (*Sarkar* Ahmadabad). A *Faujdari* with 100 *Zat* and 400 *Sawar* exists in the *Zamindari Pargana* of Mohan. (p. 216. *Sarkar Sorath*). Similarly, *Mirat* quotes the *Faujdari* appointments in various other *Parganas*.

78. *Ibid.*, I., p. 288. Despite the fact that the *Zamindari Mahal* of Port Pur Bandar was at times declared a *Khalsa* under the management of *Diwan-i Subah* and sometimes assigned in *Jagir* to any of the State officials, the Zamindar continued to get his share of 1/4th of the Port income.

3

The Zamindars of Kuch Bihar and Assam

In the *Ain's* geographical account of the *Subah* Bengal, the chief of Kutch finds mention with a contigent of 1,000 cavalry and 1000 infantry and having also under him the territory of Kamrup (*Kampta*).[1] As these territories do not find any place in any of the *Sarkars* of *Subah* Bengal, it seems that under Akbar, they remained free from the Mughal interference[2] and were brought under the Mughal control only in Jahangir's reign. After submission, Raja Parikshit Narayan was reinstated in his territory with a nominal *Jagir* but for revenue administration, the major portions of the Kamrup territory were brought under the pattern of Maghal administration.[4] Some *Parganas* were reserved in the *Khalsa*, while other were assigned in *tankwah Jagir* or assigned to the Revenue Farmers for the collection of the land revenue.[5] The territory of Kamrup was brought under the Mughal system of land revenue administration and *Karories* were appointed for the collection of the revenues in its *Parganas*.[6] Raja Lakshmi Narayan of Kamta had already submitted and having been placed under surveillance, his territory was placed under the Mughal administration.[7] Later on along with his cousin, Raja Parikshit, he was also reinstated as Zamindar with some *Jagir* by Ibrahim Khan, the Governor.[8] He helped the Imperialists in the further expansion of the Mughal territory.[9]

The *Zamindaries* of Kuch Bihar continued to exist till 1661 A.D. As Raja Bhim Narain gave shelter to the Raja of Assam, the territory of Kuch Bihar was also annexed to the Mughal State.[10] Talish also bears testimony that the land revenue administration was brought in line with the other provinces.[11] Besides this, all other petty *Zamindaries* of Kuch Bihar though continuing to exist, were inevitably brought under the Mughal pattern of administration. The contemporary evidence of late Aurangzeb's reign reveals that usually their territories were assigned in *tankhawh Jagir* to the Mughal State officials.[12]

The Zamindars of Assam

In Akbar's reign, Assam remained completely independent of the Mughal authority[13] but a portion of its Hills under the hereditary *Zamindars* was subjected by Jahangir. After reduction, the Imperial policy was not aimed at the extinction of the *Zamindars* but to enroll them in the circle of loyal *Zamindars*.[14] Though every *Zamindar* was reinstated, he was assigned only a small portion of his territory in personal *Jagir* while the rest of the territory, for the purposes of revenue administration, was attached to the Mughal administration and assigned in *Tankhawh Jagir* to the Mughal State officials.[15] Many of these Chiefs remained recalcitrant until the entire territory of Assam was annexed to the Mughal State in 1660-61 A.D. in Aurangzeb's reign.[16]

Footnotes

1. *Ain.* J. tr., p. 130. *Ain* and the other Mughal historians sometimes use the terms 'Kamrup' and 'Kamta' as synonymous. Kamta originally comprised the western part of the Brahmputtra valley upto Karatoya and was included within the kingdom of Kamrup. Both Kamrup and Kamta collectively constitute the territory of Kuch Bihar. Baharistan puts Kanrup to the east of Manas river under Raja Parikshit Narayan and Kamta to the west of the river under Raja Lakshmi Narayan. For details, see Gait's 'History of Assam,' Pp. 42-44; Baruh's '*Early History of Kamrupa*,' p. 284; B.G. tr. *Borah* II., f.n. 15, pp. 806-7.

2. *A.N. III*, 349, 1067; also *Ain*, J. tr. II., while describing the geographical limits of *Subah* Bengal comments, "Its length is 200 kos and its breath 40 to 100 kos. On the east is river Brahmaputtra, on the north is Tibet and Assam, on the South is Ghoraghat, and on the west is Tirhut." Also for details see (H.N. Chaudhari, 'Cooch Bihar State and its Land Revenue Settlements,' p. 232) Gaits, 'History of Assam' pp. 46-69; Assam Census Report, 1901, p. 382; Barua's 'Early History of Kamrupa,' pp. 284-301; Gunabhiram Baruah's Assam Buranji; Bansabali, J.A.S.B. LXII; S.K. Bhuyan's Kamrupar Buranji, pp. 6-12; also B.G. tr. Borah, II, Notes, pp. 828-29.

3. B.G. tr. I, pp. 252-53, 272, 410.

4. *Ibid.*, p. 272, 410; II, p. 521. Raja Parikshit was forced to make obedience to the corpse of the deceased Governor Islam Khan (*Ibid.*, pp. 257, 264) and presented before the new Governor Qasim Khan (*Ibid.*, pp. 292, 297, 409, 452). His territory was brought under direct Mughal administration by Qasim Khan (*Ibid.*, pp. 409-10). But later on, the next Governor Ibrahim Khan reinstated the *Raja* as a loyal Zamindar on the condition of payment of Rs. 700,000 as *Peshkash* to the Mughal State (*Ibid.*, II. p. 521).

5. *Ibid.*, I., pp. 272-73. After Raja Parikshit submitted, "Abdus Samad was appointed the Commandar of the Army at Kuch and he ordered Mirza Hasan, the *Diwan* and *Bakshi*, to arrange for the collection of the revenues in the *Parganas* and other places. The aforesaid Mirza, due to his great experience, divided the *Parganas* of the Kuch territory into 20 well defined circles, some being entrusted to the Imperial *Karories* and *Jagirdars* for realisation of revenues, some lands were given to *Mustajirs* (Revenue Farmers. *Ibid.*, pp. 272-73). Later on, the administration was entrusted to Shaykh Ibrahim Karori (*Ibid.*, p. 410) and still later given in *Jagir* to Quliji Khan, the *Sardar* (administrator) of Kuch.

6. *Ibid.*, I, pp. 288-89. A revenue officer of a *Diwan's* rank was appointed in Kuch Bihar and Kamrup and he acted under the authority of the *Diwan-i Subah* and the Governor of Bengal. After the dismissal of Mirza Hassan Mashaddi, the *Diwan* and *Bakshi* of Kuch, Mir Safi was appointed for that office. He introduced changes in the revenue assessment of all the *Parganas* of Jahangirabad but because of the excessive fixation of the assessment demand, he was also dismissed. Shaykh Ibrahim was appointed the Chief

Karori for the whole country of Kamrup. He managed the revenue and settlement affairs and Imperial Thanas were set up for this purpose in Kamrup. (*Ibid.*, p. 403)

7. B.G.I., pp. 290, 352; II 503. Of the two Rajas of Kuch Bihar, Lakshmi Narayan of Kamta division was the first to submit to the Mughal authority. For the rivalry between the two Rajas, See Gait's 'Asam', p. 65 and B.C. tr. *Borah*, II, Notes, pp. 806-7.

8. *Ibid.*, II., pp. 521.

9. *Ibid.*, pp. 589, 605, 612, 621.

10. Abul Fazl Mamuri, *Ms. Rampur*, pp. 449-450.

11. Ibriyah, *Ms. Orient*. Quart 266, Berlin, fol. 55a-55b. Rashid Khan was appointed as *Faujdar* vide fol. 13b.

12. Mufidul Insha Ms. OR 679 Bod. Oxford, fols. 17a; 22a-23a; 71a-74b; 86b-87a. Such a picture is clear from the letters of Lekh Raj, dated 1100 A.H./ 1689 A.D., which cover the working of the *Zamindari* in *Chakla* of Ghoraghat, *Sarkar* Kuch Bihar.

13. *Ain*, J. tr. II., p. 131. "Bordering on this country (Bengal) are the dominions of the Rajah of Asham (Assam) whose great pomp and state are subject of general interest."

14. B.G. tr., Borah II, pp. 566-67. Eighteen of the Hill Rajas submitted. *Ibid.*, pp. 570; 620.

15. *Ibid.*, p. 621. After his submission, Shumaruyed Kayeth was enrolled in the "circle of *Zamindars* with the gift of robe of honour" and was assigned only 20 villages for maintenance. The rest of the territory was attached to the Mughal administration. Mirza Nathan stayed at Dakhinkul and realised its revenue on behalf of the Mughal State (*Ibid.*, p. 625). Similarly, Raja Dungar Dev, Chief of Khatribhag, after reinstation was conferred only a few villages in personal *Jagir* whereas the rest of his territory was taken over for revenue administration (*Ibid.*, p. 665).

16. Mamuri, Ms. Rampur, p. 445. After conquest, its administration was put under *Qazis*, *Amins* and *Karories*.

4

The Zamindars of Bengal and Orissa

As Bengal was the first Indian Province to fall under the English occupation for administration, its *Zamindari* aspects attracted the largest discussion at the hands of his early English administrators.[1] Though in the later-Mughal period of the 18th century, the *Zamindari* system developed various new features which puzzled the English administrator scholars about its indigenous character, in principle, the main traits of the Bengal *Zamindari* system in the 16th, and more particularly in 17th century of the Mughal age, are the same as in other Provinces. After the final overthrow of the Afghan power in Bengal in 1576 A.D.[2], its territories were divided into *Khalsa* and *Jagir* recognizing at the same time the defacto position of the *Zamindars* within the pattern of the Mughal *Jagir* system. In1586 though in Bengal as in other Provinces, a uniform *Subah* administration was introduced throughout the Empire, the land revenue operations based on Mughal procedure of survey and assessment were comparatively less in Vogue.[3] *Ain* does not record the measurement tables for any of the 487 *Mahals* in 24 *Sarkars* in Bengal[4] which shows that the *Zamindaries* in all the *Sarkars* were *Ghair amli*. In Akbar's reign, the Zamindars in Bengal remained mostly turbulent and various semi-independent up-start landlords sprang up[6] and resisted the proper enforcement of the Mughal rule. Such an insecurity of the political situation casts doubt on the proper working of the *Zamindari* system based on Mughal principles and reveals a cleavage between the theory and fact of the administrative polity. It was only in the last years of Akbar and early phase of Jahangir's reign that Raja Man Singh Kachhwa and Islam Khan took stringent and effective measures for the enforcement and consolidation of the Mughal authority.[7] The real character of the working of the Mughal *Zamindari* system in Bengal and Orissa emerges only in Jahangir's reign and its picture can be clearly drawn from *Baharistan* of Mirza Nathan. As a general rule, the

Imperial policy was aimed at forcing them to submission rather than extinguishing them completely. Under the terms of submission, two-fold principle was followed towards the *Zamindars* in Bengal and Orissa. Ordinarily, such of the *Zamindars* who submitted either voluntarily or without fighting after getting an ultimatum were given back their *Zamindaries* as *Jagirs*.[9] Secondly, usually after the failure of armed resistence, major portion of the erstwhile *Zamindari* was annexed to the Mughal territory and some portion was assigned to the *Zamindar* as maintenance *Jagir*. If a *Zamindar* became rebellious, on reduction major portion of his territories were assigned in *tankhaw-jagir* to the *Mansabdars*.[10] In any case, whatever be the position of the *Zamindar* as *Jagirdar*, he had in either case to make obedience in person before the Governor and sometimes would be dispatched to the Imperial Court for submission.[11] He had to offer a near relative in surveillance as a guarantee for loyalty.[12] All loyal Zamindars had to render military service for the expansion of the Mughal Empire though some were enlisted in regular Imperial service.[13] They had essentially to pay *Peshkash*, though some paid as a nominal gift while others as regular revenues for the *Zamindari* areas other than the *Watan* or *maintenance Jagir*.[14]

After reduction to terms, the *Zamindars* of Satrajit of Bhunsa, Bir Hamir of Birlehum and Shams Khan of Pachet were restored their *Zamindaries* as *maintenance Jagir*.[15] Musa Khan, the Chief of the Bhuyans and his allies in Bhatti area were all given back full territory of their *Zamindaries* as *Jagir* with full authority for internal administration.[16] They were all obliged to pay *Peshkash* (indemnity charges) and to join the Imperialists for repelling the other rebellious Zamindars and for further expansion of the Mughal territory.[17] They had to present themselves at regular intervals at the Governor's Court.[18] Anwar Khan of Baiachung was assigned his whole territory in *Jagir* after submission, presented himself personally at Islam Khan's Court and joined the Imperialists.[19] But later on, after his rebellion, his territories were annexed and he was sent to the fort of Rohtas.[20]

As distinct from the above category, the *Zamindars* of Jessor and Bakla, though confirmed in their entire *Zamindaries,* were assigned only a portion of their territories in personal *Jagir*. The rest of the *Zamindari* territories were either assigned away to *Mansabdars* or incorporated in the *Khalsa* land. Raja Pratapaditya (of Jessor) was confirmed by Islam Khan in all his possessions and was granted the revenues of the districts of Sripur and Bikrampur in lieu of his allowance.[21] Raja Ram Chander of Bakla was put under surveillance and was assigned by Islam Khan as much of his territories as was necessary for the maintenance of his fleet; the rest of his *Zamindari* territories were given to the *Karories* and the *Jagirdars*.[22] As he proved rebellious, his entire territory was attached to the *Khalsa*. Later on during Qasim Khan's Governorship, he was reinstated in his territory with the above mentioned *Jagir*.[23] The sons of Raja Pratapaditya of Jessore also proved turbulent and were forced to submission and were sent under surveillance to the Imperial Court. But with a view to improve relations with Jessore and the European (Firingi) pirates, they were sent back and reinstated in their territory with the above mentioned *Jagir*.[24] The majority of the *Bhuyans* were placed in this class of Zamindars and were assigned only a portion of their *Zamindaries* as personal *Jagir*.

Still distinct from the 2nd category, after submission of Bayizid Karrani, the *Zamindari* of Sylhat was totally annexed to the Mughal State and was placed under the management of a Mughal administrator.[25] Though *Baharistan* mentions about the submission of the Zamindars of Kachar, Tippera and Bhalwa, it does not say anything about the nature of their *Jagirs*. The very fact that the Mughal Thanas were established therein[26] suggests that either like Sylhat, they were totally annexed or a major portion of their territories was put under direct administration and they were left only with small *Jagirs*.

As regards the land revenue administration, it is clear that as such of the *Zamindaries* which were entrusted in *Jagir* in entirety were declared *Ghair amli*, and the *Zamindars* were left with autonomy for revenue administration. But such of the *Zamindaries*, whereof only small portions were assigned for personal *Jagir* to their Chiefs, were declared *amli* subject to the Mughal procedure of assessment and collection of revenues. In case of *Zamindari* of Bakla, Baharistan notes that apart from the personal *Jagir* assigned to Raja Ram Chander, the rest of the territories were given to the *Karories* and the *Jagirdars*[27] who under the Mughal rules were bound to get them assessed based on regular survey and record-of-rights. Similarly, in Jessore, the Raja was given a small *Jagir* and its territories were placed under direct Mughal administration. Khwaja Mohammad Tahir deputed to assess the revenues of Jessore prepared the '*Jama*' (assessment) document bearing the signatures of the *Chaudharies* and the *Qanungos* and was consequently enforced on the *Ryots* and the *Jagirdars* for the revenue realisations.[28] Apart from this, the *Zamindaries* totally annexed to the Mughal State were essentially declared *amli*. This is borne out by Baharistan's detailed narration of the revenue operations enforced in Sylhat.[29]

Though Dr. Ray Chaudhari concedes the fact that during the Governorship of Islam Khan and Qasim Khan, 'the semi-independent princelings were all reduced to the position of *Jagirdars* or subordinate

Zamindars and 'some also become officers of the Mughal Empire,'[30] he considers the position anomalous. He further points out that Ibrahim Khan's policy of reconciliation ended this anomaly and that more or less uniform relationship was now established between the Mughal Government and the Zamindars who became full fledged vassals of the Empire. The restoration of territories was no longer nominal but real.[31] Dr. Chaudhari forgets that the variation in treatment of the Zamindars in the initial stages of conquest was inevitable in the face of the doubtful allegiance and oft-repeated recalcitrance on the part of certain Zamindars. [32] By Ibrahim Khan's time, the situation had comparatively settled down and the Mughal court decided to set free the Princes kept under surveillance and reinstated the Chiefs of Jessore and Kuch. But the restoration of the *Zamindaries* never meant any recognition of the Chiefs as semi-independent with only nominal allegiance to the Mughal State. Even their *Jagir* grant never comprised the full territories of their respective *Zamindaries* but only a part thereof, the rest still remaining with the Mughal officers for revenue administration. Moreover, the Chiefs also remained subject to the Mughal *Zamindari* regulations of allegiance and military service. The policy of Ibrahim Khan later on followed towards the Chiefs of Kuch Bihar, Kamrup and Assam Hills clearly suggests that the *Zamindars* were left only with a portion of *Zamindari* territory in personal *Jagir* and it could not have been otherwise in the already consolidated areas in Bengal. The final policy pursued towards the Bengal *Zamindars* was not exceptional but was exactly in line with the general policy adopted in other Provinces.

After its consolidation in Bengal, simultaneous with the pre-Mughal hereditary Chiefs and *Bhuyans*, the Mughal Government also created a new class of official Zamindars who like their counterparts in other Provinces, were assigned *Jagirs* in lieu of the discharge of police duties and collection of revenues in their territories. Such *Zamindaries* were essentially *amli* and the revenue realizations were always deposited as *Peshkash* with the Mughal State. Though Dr. Chaudhari has rightly traced the distinct existence of such a *Zamindari* class,[34] his assertion for the autonomous character for every category of *Zamindari* is completely erroneous.[35] The Zamindars, of course, exercised police, judicial and financial powers for the collection of the revenues but except in a *Ghair amli* territory, the hereditary chiefs were never vested with assessment powers. Their *amli* territories and the territories of the official *Zamindars* were always assessed by the Mughal officials. Despite errors in some respects, Grant's analysis on the Zamindar's role in the Mughal revenue administration is nearer the truth.[36] Moreland's criticism of Grant is not justified and his view that the Zamindars paid a fixed lump sum unassessed amount to the State is based on his wrong reading of the *Ain*.[37] Even if Moreland's analysis of the *Ain* is accepted, it connot be asserted that the nature of land revenue administration in the *Zamindaries* of unsettled Bengal as under Akbar remained static throughout the Mughal age. With the gradual consolidation of the Mughal authority from Jahangir's reign onwards, it can be maintained on the basis of fresh contemporary evidence not available to Moreland, that by and large *Ghair amli* territories of the *Zamindaries* were rendered *amli*. More than Baharistan for Jahangir's time, *Murraqat-i Hasan* and *Ibriya of Talish* completely bear it out for the reigns of Shahjahan and Aurangzeb.[38] In principle, the *Zamindari* system in Bengal worked on the same lines as in other Provinces. Mirza Mohammad Hadi's and Murshid Quli's revenue reforms marked the culmination of the process of integration in the realm of land revenue administration.[39] Dr. Chaudhri, in view of the evidence from Baharistan, has rightly criticized Moreland's tentative picture of identifying the Zamindars with the revenue Farmers paying fixed sums by way of demand.[40] Though he makes correct distinction between the Zamindars paying *Peshkash* and the revenue Farmers, his own conclusion that the land belonging to the Zamindars was not assessed stands true only for the *Ghair amli* territory. In fact, as already noted, despite radical difference in the nature of their respective possessions, the *amli* territory with the Zamindars and the land with the revenue Farmers were both subject to regular methods of Mughal assessment.

Zamindars in Orissa

Both *Ain* and *Baharistan* refer to the existence of numerous widespread *Zamindars* in Orissa under Akbar and Jahangir.[41] Of the Chief Zamindars, Raja Ram Chander Deb was recognised by Man Singh in 1580 A.D. when the latter was commissioned by Raja Todar Mal for the survey of Orissa lands.[42] But it seems that like the Bengal Chiefs, the Orissa Zamindars were equally turbulent. Under Jahangir, Raja Purushottam Deb, son of Ram Chander Deb, submitted to the Mughal authority and undertook to pay tribute (*Peshkash*) and gifts (*Nalbandi*).[43] As the Chief was habitually recalcitrant, in 1611 A.D., he was reduced by Raja Kalyan and finally in 1617 A.D., his territories were annexed to the Imperial dominion.[44] Salim Khan, the Zamindar of Hijli was suppressed in Jahangir's reign but was restored his territory as *Jagir*.[45] The other Chiefs were also reduced and the fact on Shah Jahan's rebellion, they were honored on submission shows their 'defacto' recognition.[46] *Murraqat-i Hassan* provides us with a detailed account of the working of the *Zamindari* system under Shah Jahan and the beginning of Aurangzeb's reign.[47] By that time the Zamindars had been reduced to the status of more tax-gatherers paying lumpsum *Peshkash* (*Zar Peshkash-i Muqarari*) fixed in installments after every crop.[47] The *Peshkash* was realised by the *Diwan* through the *Faujdar* or was assigned in *Tankwah Jagir* to the *Jagirdars* who realised it through their own machinery of collection. The *Zamindaries* were invariably *amli* subject to regular assessment. The *Peshkash* was based on regular assessment done by the *Amin* with the help of the local *Qanungos* and the *Chaudharies*. The assessment documents were attested by the Zamindars and the other local officials.

Footnotes

1. *Collected Works of Professor B.R. Grover, Vol. III, Indian Agrarian Structure: Ancient to Early British: Elements of Continuity and Change*, Edited by Amrita Grover, Dr. Anju Grover Chaudhary, Dr. J C Dua, Delhi, 2007, pp. 183-210.

2. A.N. tr. Bev., pp. 248-49.

3. See discussion on the 'Nasq' in Bengal', Collected Works, *op. cit.*, pp. 167-174.

4. *Ain* J. II. pp. 142-157.

5. A.N. tr. Bev. pp. 251-52, *Ain* J. II. p. 130 makes an implied statement that in East Bengal (Bhatti), the Mughal Government was content with its formal recognition. It comments, "The tract of country on the east called Bhati, is reckoned a part of this Province. It is ruled by Isa Afghan and the *Khutba* is read and the Coin struck in the name of the present Majesty." According to *Ain*, the Bhatti region comprised the eastern portions of Deccan.

6. The *Bhuyans* comprised a set of powerful Chiefs who rose to power after the fall of Daud, the last Karrani Sultan of Bengal in 1576 A.D. Mirza Nathan puts their number at twelve which is approximate rather than exact. Of the numerous minor Zamindars who fought against Islam Khan under the leadership of Musa Khan, son of Isa Khan and his ally Usman, Nathan does not specifically mention which of these the *Bunyans* were. For further discussion on *Bhuyans*, see Dr. Wise, Bara Bhuyans, J.A.S.B., 1824, pp. 197-214; Blochmann, J.A.S.B., 1873, 223, and his *Ain*, I, p. 342 Beveridge, J.A.S.B., 1904, p. 57; B.G. tr. Borah, II; Notes pp. 799-800; also Chauduri T.R., 'Bengal under Akbar and Jahangir, pp. 1-3.

7. Raja Man Singh was Governor of Bengal from A.N. tr. Bev. pp. 269-70. Islam Khan was the Governor from 1608 A.D. to 1613 A.D. For details, see Borah's introduction to *Baharistan* I, pp. xiv-xviii, Chaudhari T.R. 'Bengal', pp. 1-5.

8. B.G. tr. II, p. 566.

9. *Ibid*, I., p. 18. Islam Khan sent Iftikhar Khan against Satrajit of Bhunsa with the instruction that if the latter submitted, he should be given the hope of his territory as *Jagir*, otherwise his country should be left as a prey to the horse of the Imperial *Karoris*.

10. *Ibid.*, II., p. 518.

11. *Ibid.*, pp. 566-67.

12. *Ibid.*, I., p. 100.

13. *Ibid.*, I, p. 100; II. pp. 517, 522, 568.

14. *Ibid.*, I, p. 123; II. pp. 521-22.

15. *Ibid.*, pp. 18-20, 327. For geographical situation of these territories, see Rennell's Map. No.7; also tr. Borah. Notes pp. 800-801.

16. *Ibid,* p. 100. After the surrender of Musa Khan and his allies, "the estate of each of them was back to them as Jagir for their maintenance." For geographical situation of Bhatti Chieftainships, See J.B.O.R.S., IV, p. 18; *Bengal: Past and Present*, 1928, xxxv, 33 and xxxviii, p. 25; also tr. Borah II., p. 796.

17. *Ibid*, pp. 19, 29, 319.

18. *Ibid*, p. 327. "When, of all the Zamindars, Shams Khan, Zamindar of Birbhum, Bir Hamir, Zamindar of Pachet and Bahadur Khan, newphew of Salim Khan Hijliwal did not present themselves (at the Governor Court), Shaykh Kamal was dispatched against Shams Khan and Bir Hamir."

19. *Ibid.*, p. 105.

20. *Ibid.*, p. 140.

21. *Ibid.*, p. 28. Jessore is included in the *Ain* as Mahal of Sarkar Khalifatbad. (Ain. J. tr. II, p. 134) Bahristan mentions it as 'Jasar'.

22. *Ibid.*, p. 132.

23. *Ibid.*, II, p. 521.

24. *Ibid.*

25. *Ibid.*, p. 208; Mukarram Khan was appointed as *Sardar* (Adminstrator) of the whole *Sarkar* of Sylhat (pp. 326-27). Later on Mirza Nathan, the author of Baharistan was himself appointed the *Sardar* of Sylhat. (*Ibid.* II., p. 633). *Ain.* J. II. p. 152 mentions Sylhat as a *Sarkar* division with 8 *Mahals* in *Subah* Bengal. For details, see Sylhat D.G p. 11; Geographical situation, Rennel's Map 6; tr. Borah, Notes, p. 819.

26. *Ibid.*, II., p. 690.

27. *Ibid.*, p. 132.

28. *Ibid.*, pp. 156-57 "Khwaja Muhammad Tahir, who went to Jessore to assess its revenues, returned to Islam Khan with the register of revenue of that country, which was prepared to the satisfaction of the *Ryots* and to the advantage of the Imperial treasury. It was presented to Islam Khan with the signatures of the *Chaudhries* and *Qanungos*; it was then handed over to the accountants of Mutaqid Khan in order to enforce these regulations on the *Ryots* and the *Jagirdars*."

29. *Ibid.*, 326-27; II p. 633.

30. Dr. Chaudhari's '*Bengal*', p. 18.

31. *Ibid.*, p. 20.

32. Even after submission, rebellion against the Mughal authority was quite frequent on the part of some Zamindars. For details, See B.G.I. pp. 32, 105-6; 127, 131, 134, 136, 139; II 623-25, 639, 782.

33. *Ibid.*, II., p. 521.

34. Chaudhari, '*Bengal*', pp. 20-21.

35. *Ibid.*, pp. 21-23. Dr. Chaudhari has been misled by Grant's analysis regarding the powers of the Zamindars. In fact, the exercise of administrative powers inherent in the *Zamindari* institution itself did not imply any autonomy, least of all in the sphere of land revenue administration. In this respect, further distinction has to be made for the powers of every category of Zamindar. In face of the blurred position of the working of the *Zamindari* in the 18th century which tended to mitigate distinction between different categories of the Zamindars and the Mughal State revenue officials the views of Grant and Westland, though true mostly for the 18th century, cannot be wholly applicable to the 17th century Bengal. For early Aurangzeb's period, Talish's continuation of *Ibriya* (Bod. Oxford. Fols. 118a-119a) clearly mentions the revenue realisations of the *Khalsa, Jagir* and the *Gima* lands based on measurement operations in practically the whole of Bengal excepting Chittagong (fol. 164a) which had been entered by the *Qanungos* as *Ghair-amli* ever since the Mughal conquest and always assigned in *tankhwa Jagir* to the *Mansabdars*.

36. Grant's Survey, 29-30, 32-33, 172. Grant's 'Historical and Comparative Analysis', vide Firminger's 'The Fifth Repot' p. II, p. 170, "It is further advanced as incontrovertible, that the Zamindars or other classes of natives, hithero considered the rightful proprietors of the lands, are no more than annual contracting farmers or receivers of the public rents, with stated allowances in the nature of a commission on the receipts, and a small estate or portions of their territorial jurisdictions set apart for constant family subsistence, whether in or out of office, but never exceeding in the whole, by a universal prescriptive law of the empire, 10% on the Muffusil collections."

37. Moreland, 'Agrarian system', Pp. Appendix G. Moreland's difficulty arises from his rigid concept of the *Ain's* statistics of revenue tables denoting valuation rather than 'demand' (See discussion on 'Tabti system'), his interpretation of 'Nasq' (See discussion on 'Nasq') and his belief to the effect, "As time went on, the distinction between Chiefs, Farmers and Officials disappeared, because there was, in fact, no difference in the incidence of the various positions, and all alike came to be known as Zamindars." The latter view is true only for the mid-eighteenth century and not for the 17th century and early 18th century until after Murshid Quli's revenue reforms which make a clear cut traditional distinction between different categories of revenue officials and the Zamindars. (For Murshid Quli's reforms, See 18th century Histories of Bengal, viz. Riazul Salatin, Pers. text. pp. 252-53.

38. Murraqat-i Hasan, Rampur, pp. 17-18. Apart from these contemporary sources, Riazul Salatin (*Ibid*, pp. 26-27) 18th century Bengal History giving details of the revenue reforms of Mirza Mohammad Hadi, Diwan of Bengal in Aurangzeb's reign, states that assessment documents of the *Khalsa, Jagir* and *Zamindari* lands of all the *Parganas* and *Mahals* were prepared afresh based on survey and measurement operations. Also, see *Tarikh-i Bangala*, Ms. 1038 Tarikh, Asifiya Hyderabad, fols. 14a-15b.

39. Mirza Mohammad Hadi, (vide R.S. *Ibid.*; Tariki Bengal, *Ibid.*,) and expert in the revenue and *Faujdari* affairs was appointed *Diwan* of Orissa and later on was transferred by Aurangzeb as *Diwan* of *Subha* Bengal. Mirza Hadi enforced revenue reforms for the preparation of assessments based on survey and measurement and the state regulations in all categories of land inclusive of the *Zamindari* territories. He confirmed the assignments of the Zamindars as *tankhawh Jagir*. The Zamindars were enjoined to be extremely regular and punctual in the realisation of the land revenues and to look after the interests of the *ryots*. In Bengal, Murshid Quli reinforced the revenue reforms and regulations and like Mirza Hadi screwed up the machinery of the *Zamindari* institution. Dr. Chaudhari thinks that Murshid Quli "merely put the Zamindars under a binding obligation to pay their revenues regularly. Even this sole mark of bondage had apparently been ignored in the preceeding years, when Mughal authority is supposed to have been most firmly entrenched in Bengal" and that the Zamindars "were certainly the masters of the situation within their estates"......... He concludes, "The Zamindars, within their territories were free to rule as they liked: free to rule, and free to oppress." (vide 'Bengal', pp. 22, 42). Dr. Chaudhari has completely failed to understand the working of the institution of *Zamindari* in Bengal. Whereas the police, administrative and revenue powers were inherent in the institution of *Zamindari*, the revenue powers were more of an obligation than a privilege and were always subject to the State regulations of Survey and assessment. Dr. Chaudhari is inconsistent and shifty in his arguments. When face to face with *Baharistan* and the original Mughal documents, he is inclined to believe that the Zamindars were reduced to the status of *Jagirdars* and tax gatherers but while banking on the later family annals and Bengali literature (*Ibid.*, pp. 19, 22-3; Bibliography. p. 236), he believes in the complete autonomy and unrestrained revenue powers of the Zamindars. Similarly, while analyzing the Mughal *Farman* of Shahan Jahan's reign concerning a *Zamindari* appointment, Dr. Chaudhari recognizes that in return for his privileges, the Zamindar "was required to be punctilious in his remittances of revenue and to look after the welfare of the people." (*Ibid.* p. 21). On the other hand, without realising the implications of the conditional grant or confirmation of personal *Jagir* of a Zamindar, and without any substantial contemporary evidence, Dr. Chaudhari jumps to the conclusion that the obligation of the revenue duties was a mark of bondage which was always ignored by the Zamindar during the Mughal rule (*Ibid.*, p. 22).

40. *Ibid.*, pp. 47-48.

41. *Ain.* J. tr. II. pp. 155-57.

42. B.G. tr. II, Notes, p. 806. Raja Chander Deb's "territory included a large area extending from Mahanadi (the northern boundry of Cuttak) to Khemti near Gaujam. He was also appointed the hereditary guardian of the temple of Jagannath." Also for details, see Stirling, Asiatic Researches, XV, p. 294; Hunter, Orissa, II, p. 190; L.M. Ghosh, 'Indian Chiefs,' p. 450.

43. *Ibid.*, I. P. 37. The Raja paid *Peshkash* (tribute) of Rupees three hundred thousand and was paid to the Mughal Emperor besides *Nal Bandi* (small gift) of Rupees One hundred thousand and his daughter in marriage to the conquering Chiefs Raja Keshodas Maru, the Mughal *Mansabdar*. For the latter's Career, see tr. Borah. Notes, p. 806.

44. *Tuzk-i Jahangiri*, Pers. text. pp. 193, 214-15.

45. B.G. tr. I, pp. 18-20, 327. Also 'Diary of Abdul Latif' discovered and published by J.N. Sarkar in *Prabasi*. 1326 B.S. pp. 552-53.

46. *Ibid.*, II , p. 688.

47. *Muraqat-i Hassan* Ms. Rampur, pp. 107-8, 261-62, 272-73.

5

Zamindars in Rajasthan

All the pre-mughal independent or semi-independent Rajput chiefs in Rajasthan were brought under the Mughal pattern of the *Zimmidari* administration. Akbar's policy of imperialism led him to subdue the Rajasthan Chiefs but guided by the political expediency for the stability and consolidation of the Empire, he scrupulously refrained from the total annexation of the territories of the Rajput Chiefs. The coexistence of loyal hereditary *Zimmidars* was by no means incompatible with this concept of Imperial polity. Each one of them was enrolled as the *Mansabdar* of the Mughal State and in lieu of the millitry services, was confirmed in his *Zimmidari* comprising the *Watan* (patrimony) and other *jagir* lands awarded in accordance with the *mansab* value. At times, even other *Mansabdars* of their personal family or tribe were also awarded *mansabs* and *jagirs*. Excepting Mewar, which was often recalcitrant, invariably all of them remained loyal to the Mughal State and fromed the backbone of the Mughal nobility.

Amber

The chiefs of Amber, Jodhpur, Ranthambhor (Boondi), Bikaner, Jaisalmer, Siroh, Banswarah, Jalor and Dungarpur accepted Akbar's supremacy.[1] Despite the Mughal occupation of the major portions of Mewar, Rana Udai Singh and his successor, Rana Pratap, did not acknowledge Akbar's authority[2] but later in Jahangir's reign, Rana Karan Singh acepted the Mughal supremacy.[3] In Akbar's reign, the Kachhwah Raja Bihari Mal of Amber was the first to recognise the Mughal supremacy and was awarded the rank of 5000.[4] Amber chiefs must have been subject to the rulers of Marawars, mentioned as one of the 28 *mahals* of Sarkar Ajmer-but its area covered title over 1/5th of its total area.[5] His successors Raja Bhagwan Dass (under Akbar), Raja Man Singh, Mirza Rana Bhao

Singh with 5000 *mansabs*[6] Raja Maha Singh (under Jahangir), Mirza Raja Jai Singh[7]; Raja Ram Singh[8], Bishen Singh,[9] and Sawae Jai Singh (under Aurangzeb)[10] worked as high profile *Mansabdars* under the Mughal Empire.

After the submission, the principality of Amber was included in the *Sarkar* of Ajmer. The *watan jagir* comprised only the single *Pargana* of Amber which always remained with the family throughout the Mughal age.[11] The Amber Chiefs held high *mansabs* and numerous *tankhwa jagirs* were attached to the ruling princes from time to time.

Jodhpur

Chander Sain, driven out by the Mughal forces from Marwar submitted at Nagor but again rebelled.[12] The Rathor ruler of Marwar (Jodhpur), Udai Singh,[13] acknowledged the Mughal supremacy in 1584 A.D.[14] and got *gaddi* in 1587 A.D.[15] He was given the title of *Raja* with a *mansab* of 1000 *zat & sawar.*[16] Raja Sur Singh acknowledged the Mughal supremacy during the period of Akbar and Jahangir.[17] Later, Gaj Singh enjoyed a *mansab* of 3000 *zat* and 2000 *sawar* with a standard and title of *Raja* during the period of Jahangir and Shahjahan.[18] The same position was enjoyed by Jaswant Singh.[19] After him, Rajasthan was totally annexed to the Mughal State.[20] Ajit Singh, the minor, succeeded and was given 1500 *zat* & 5000 *sawar* and *jalor* in *jagir.*[21]

Much less realised hitherto, the Marwar principality of Jodhpur constituted a Sarkar division of Gujrajt Sultanate in the pre-Mughal era[22] and the Rajput Chiefs of Jodhpur were entitled to only one fourth area as *watan jagir* whereas the rest of the area (*Talpad*) was considered a part of the *Khalsa* territory of the Sultanate. In lieu of the *watan-jagir*, the Jodhpur chief rendered the military service of 3000 *sawar* to Ghazni Khan, son of Malik Khanji Jalori, the Chief assignee of the territory.[23] (the total revenues both of *watan jagir* and *Talpad* 2 Lacs 75 Rs). After the Mughal conquest, the entire *Sarkar* of Jodhpur was transferred to *Subah* Ajmer. Though the Jodhpur chiefs were enrolled as *Mansabdars*, as amongst the Mughal nobility, their *watan jagir* was confirmed with status quo whereas the other portions of the *Sarkar* divisions were regarded as directly administered territories of the Mughal State. A portion from this was assigned for the Jodhpur chiefs only if warranted by the *jagir* regulations in accordance with the *mansab* awarded. In 1678 A.D. (Aurangzeb's reign) after the death of Maharaja Jaswant Singh, the *Zimmidari* of Jodhpur was annexed to the Mughal Empire over the disputed question to the Gaddi succession.[24] Ajmer Singh, the posthumous son, was not recognised as the *Zimmidar* but was awarded an ordinary *jagir* in Jalor (S.Sirohi) in lieu of the *mansab* 1500 *zats* and 5000 *sawars*.[25]

Nagor

Like Jodhpur, Nagor also constituted a *Sarkar* of Gujrat Sultanate[26] and after Mughal conquest was formed a *Sarkar* division of *Subah* Ajmer. *Zimmidars* in Nagor, the Hada Rajputs in lieu of their services for the improvement and colonisation in the territories held half of the *Parganas* in *Zimmidari* and were entitled to 1/4th of share from the revenues of the villages within their *Zimmidaris*. In lieu of their income, they had to supply a fixed contigent of 200 *sawars* to Khazni Khan[27]- total income, Rs, 2,55,000. After the Mughal conquest, they were confirmed with status quo though in lieu of rendering fixed contigent, they were awarded corresponding *mansabs*. The *Zimmidaries* of Dungarpur, Banswara and Sirohi and Jalor constituted a full *Sarkar* each under the Gujrat Sultanate[28] and each *Zimmidari* claimed only one fourth as *watan jagir* and the rest of the territory was assignable to any other State assignee. After the Mughal conquest, they were all grouped under one *Sarkar* of *Sirohi* of *Subah* Ajmer under Akbar.[29] and each *Zimmidari* was continued with status quo. Apart from the *watan jagir*, the three-fourth portion of each *Zimmidari* was assignable to any other *Jagirdar* if not assigned to the *Zimmidars* themselves in lieu of *mansab*. At times, these *Zimmidari* areas were held in *tankhwa jagir* by the *Zimmidars* themselves which sometimes were assigned in *tankhwa jagirs* to the Mewar Chiefs, who otherwise, too claimed their historical right of supremacy over them.[30]

Bikaner

The Bikaner chief Kalyan Singh accepted Akbar's authority in 1570.[31] His successor, Rao Rai Singh and his brother were enrolled as *Mansabdars*.[32] However, Jahangir was not too happy with Rao Rai Singh and transferred him first to Deccan and thereafter to Burhanpur.[33] Jahangir conferred *gaddi* later to Dalpat Singh (1611-13).[34] When Dalpat Singh rebelled against the Mughal Emperor, his younger brother Suraj Singh was sent against him. Dalpat Singh was defeated and slained. Thereafter, Suraj Singh got *gaddi* with a *mansab* of 4000 *zat* and 4000 *sawar*.[35] Afterwards, Karan Singh (1631-69), who had sided with Aurangzeb in the war of succession, was conferred a *mansab* of 2000 *zat* and 1500 *sawar* with *Rao's* title. Later, Karan Singh was transferred to Deccan by Aurangzeb and *gaddi* was conferred on Anup Singh with a *mansab*.[36] Swarup Singh and Sajjan Singh served Aurangzeb faithfully.[37]

After conquest, the *Zimmidari* of Bikaner along with other areas was formed into a full *Sarkar*. The *watan jagir* comprised the *pargana* of Bikaner while the members of the family also held other *jagir* lands in lieu of their services.

Jaisalmer

The Batti ruler of Jaisalmer, Rawal Bhim Singh, accepted Akbar's authority and held *mansab* under him.[38] He held a *mansab* of 500. His son, Rawal Kalyan Singh, was recognised and awarded a *mansab* of 2000 *zats*, 1000 *sawars*.[39] His successors, Subbal Singh, Umra Singh and Jaswant Singh served under Shahjahan and Aurangzeb.[40]

The principality of Jaisalmer comprised the *watan jagir* of *Pargana* Jaisalmer (S. Bikaner).[41] Apart from the *watan jagir*, the ruling princes held other *jagirs* too in lieu of the services rendered, Tod[42] thinks that from the time of accession of Subbul Singh to the *gaddi* (vide Shah Jahan's reign) the *Zimmidari* of Jaisalmer became a fief of the Mughal Empire with a considerably decreased territorial jurisdiction. Tod comments,[43] "This was the first considerable abstraction from the territories which had been progressively increased by Rawal Jaisal and his successors (pre-Mughal era) but which have since been woefully curtailed. A short time before Babur's invasion, the dependencies of Jaisalmer extended on the north to the Gara River, west to the Mihram Indus; and on the east and the south they were bounded by the Rathors of Bikaner and Marwar who had been gradually encroaching for two centuries, and continue to do so to this day. The entire *thal* of Barmer Kotra, in the south, were Bhatti chieftainships, and eastward to the site of Bikaner itself." Dr. Saran, basing on Jahangir's statement about the grant of territories of Jaisalmer to Rawal Kalyan as *tankhwa jagir* in lieu of the *mansab* awarded, considers that Jaisalmer had already been degraded from its earlier status of a subordinate vassal to that of a *jagir*, held by the Chief as equivalent of his salary. Though both Tod and Dr. Saran are correct in their statement of the Jaisalmer being held as *tankhaw jagir*, they have failed to realise that this had been true ever since the principality submitted to the Mughal State in Akbar's reign. In principle, the treatment meted out to Jaiselmer was not exceptional and can be put at par with any other *Zimmidari*, Amber, Bikaner, Jodhpur excepting the chiefs of the latter were usually awarded much larger *tankhaw jagirs* in lieu of their *mansabs* and services.[44]

Ranthambhor (Bundi)

In pre-Akbar's era, the Hara Chauhans of Ranthambhor owed suzerainity to Rana of Mewar.[45] In 1599, Raja Surajan Singh surrendered to Akbar and accepted his authority.[46] Though enrolled as *Mansabdar*, the Hara Chiefs were exempted from branding, not to go beyond Attock and not to serve under a Hindu Chief.[47] Later on, Raja Surjan Singh was conferred with the title, '*Rao Raja*' of Boondi[48] and also appointed as commander to reduce *gondwana*.[49] His successor, Rao Bhoj Singh, served

Akbar in his campaign against Surat. He was also appointed Governor of Garh, Kantanga and subsequently, of Chunargarh.[50] Later, Rao Bhoj fell out of Akbar's favour.[51] However, his successor, Rao Rattan, was granted the title of '*Rao Rai*' with a *mansab* of 5000.[52] He served both Jahangir and Shahjahan and held the post of governor of Burhampur. His successor, Chuttersal, served Shahjahan and was declared Governor of the Imperial capital and held high office under Aurangzeb.[53] Raja of Bundi kept neutral in the war of succession. He was killed in *Samwat* 1715. Aurangzeb was not happy with his successor, Rao Bhao, but later reconciled.[54] His successor, Anurag Singh (1738 *Samwat*, 1682 A.D.), served Aurangzeb in Deccan war. Thereafter, Boodh Singh succeeded his father, Anurag Singh, and served Aurangzeb.[55]

After its conquest, the principality of Ranthambor was constituted into a full-fledged *sarkar* Division of Ajmer. The *watan jagir* of the ruling family of Ranthambor was confirmed in the Pargana of Bundi.

Bundi

As the family members of Bundi were enlisted amongst the nobility, and played conspicuous role in the Mughal wars, they usually held larger *jagirs* of other *Parganas* adjacent to the *watan jagir*.[56]

Kotah

An offshoot of the Haras of Ranthambor and Bundi-Madhava Singh, the second son of Rattan Singh was assigned Kotah & Phalista with a *mansab* of 2500 *zat* & 1500 *sawar*. Thereafter, Kotah was established as a separate State by Shahjahan[57] and it became a hereditary *Zimmidari*.[58] His son, Mukand Singh, succeeded the throne during the 21st regnal year of Shahjahan and was given a *mansab* of 2000 *zats*, 1500 *sawars* and *watan jagir*.[59] Jagat Singh, son of Mukand Singh, served in Aurangzeb's reign and was given a *mansab* of 2000 and *watan jagir*. Kishor Singh succeeded Jagat Singh.[60] Thereafter, Ram Singh, son of Kishore Singh, was conferred a *watan jagir* and a *gaddi* with 4000 *zat* and 4000 *sawar*.[61]

The *Zimmidari* of Kotah comprising the *watan jagir* of the *pargana* of Kotah (*Sarkar* Ranthambor) originated in (?) A.D. based on the Mughal *altamgha jagir* grant.[62] The creation of this *Zimmidari* is a classical example illustrating the relationship between the royal prerogative and a princely *Zimmidari*. In lieu of their services, the *Zimmidars* of this family held other *Jagirs* apart from the *watan jagir*.

Mewar

Founded on the basis of traditional family honour and helped by the geographical situation, the Sisodia chiefs of Mewar comparatively asserted independent spirit in their relationship with the Mughal Empire. Despite the fall of Chittor in Haldighat and the Mughal occupation of the major portions of Mewar and various campaings, Maharaja Udai Singh and his successor, Rana Pratap, did not accept Akbar's authority and established new capital at Udaipur in region of the huge Kaywen.[63] Ultimately, in 1615, after prolonged warfare, realising the futility of further resistance to the Mughal forces[64] and with Jahangir's offer of moderate conciliatory peace terms, Rana Amar Singh accepted the Mughal supremacy. The Maharana's son, K.Karan Singh, was enrolled as the *Mansabdar* of the Mughal State (5000 *zats & sawars*) as a noble of the Mughal Court but exempted from personal attendance at the Court. The Maharana was to supply a contingent of 1000 *sawars* and was confirmed in the *watan jagir* and awarded huge *jagir* lands.[65]

Though the succeeding Mewar chiefs formally recognised the Mughal supremacy and remained subject to the Mughal regulations of the *Zimmidari* system, a few of these, especially Rana Sagar, remained recalcitrant at heart and at finding any opportune moment asserted indifference to the Mughal control. In violation of the peaceful obligations, they made repeated, though futile, attempts to repair the fortifiction of Chittor and exacted allegiance from the erstwhile vassal chiefs of Mewar. But the Mughal government enforced upon them the supply of the military contingent and the *jagir* regulations. After submission, Rana Amar Singh, in accordance with the treaty, took Chittor back from Rana Sagar except for a small incident that Rana Amar singh forcibly occupied the *jagirs* of Begum of Rattangarh from Shekhawat Narian Dass, assignee of Rana Sagar. This was out of enmity with Rana Sagar who had held the possession of Chittor earlier. Jahangir awarded him *jagir* near Ajmer. The relations between Udaipur and Delhi remained extremly cordial during the periods of Amar Singh and Karan Singh. In the latter period, Shah Jahan even appointed Qazi Mulla Jamal as the Royal Qazi at Udaipur.[66]; Rana Jagat Singh (1628-1642 A.D.)[67] attempted repatriation of the Chittor Fort and devastated the *Zimmidaries* of Devuya, Dungarpur, Banswara and Sirohi for asserting the pre-Akbar supremacy of Mewar[68] but later on tendered apology to Shahjahan for pardon. He was dispatched with Bhopat Ram of Dharyavad along with contingent to Deccan.[69] He sent K. Raj Singh with presents to Shahjahan near Ajmer.[70] Even his younger brother, Gharib Dass, was enrolled as a *Mansabdar* with 1500 *zat* 700 *sawar*[71] and later Rai Singh, son of Hari Das Jhala, *Jagirdar* of Sadri was given a *mansab* of 1000 *zat* and 400 *sawar*.[72]

Of all the Mewar chiefs, Rana Raj Singh (1652-1680 A.D.), was the shrewdest and as an opportunist, defied and accepted the Mughal authority in accordance with the circumstances. He took up the repair of the Chittor Fort but gave up the plan after Shahjahan's march to Ajmer and Sadda Ullah Khan's campaign against Chittor and apologized.[73] But he later on devastated some of the Mughal Khalsa *Parganas* in Mewar and the *Zimmidars* of Shahpura. Thereafter, he exploited the situation of the jealousy amongst the sons of Shahjahan and got commitments for further *jagirs* from Aurangzeb. His *jagir* was confirmed by Aurangzeb and he was promised the *Pargana* of Pur, Maundal and Badnorctc.[74] But later on, after the imposition of *jizzya*, his relations with Aurangzeb became quite strained.[75] He gave shelter to the Rathore Ajit Singh of Marwar. Mughals declared war against Mewar.[76] Aurangzeb personally marched into Mewar.[77] After Rana Raj Singh's death in war, his successor Rana Jai Singh (1680-1681) formed an alliance with the rebel Prince Akbar and Durga Das Rathore of Jodhpur against Aurangzeb. Dyal Shah, one of the ministers of the Rana, revaged Sarangpur, Devas, Sironj, Mandu, Ujjain, etc, and caused devastation (1680 December).[78] Rana of Mewar and Rathores helped Prince Akbar and installed him as Emperor at Nadole. Upon failure of Akbar's conspiracy, Prince Azam was sent against Rana Jai Singh and the latter was forced to sign a treaty. He was awarded a *mansab* of 500 *zat & sawar* and *Parganas* of Mandal, etc. However, Mandal was taken back in lieu of *jaziya* and the rest of the territories were given back to Mewar.[79] Mughal Supremacy was acknowledged in Rana's letter to Aurangzeb.[80] His successor, Rana Amar Singh II (1698-1707), except for some earlier attitude in the disputed *parganas* of Mawalgarh,[81] fully submitted to the Mughal administration[82] and sent a contigent of troops to participate in Aurangzeb's war in the Deccan.[83]

Despite all assertions for the independence or nominal vassalage of Mewar to the Mughals, the fact remains that the Mewar Chiefs did not own the entire pre-Mughal territory and that in the agrarian setup, they stood in same relationship to the Mughal State as any other Rajasthan Chief. Under Akbar, the very cause for the non-acceptance of the Mughal supremacy resulted in the annexation of the entire Mewar principality to the Mughal territory and was constituted as the *Sarkar* of Chittor in *Subah* Ajmer.[84] In actual fact, Mewar came to be partitioned with indeterminate fluctuating boundary, with major portions under the Mughal control and the territory confined to Girwa hill in the south-west of Mewar. Rana Pratap redeemed his position in the south-west Bhill territory, Kumkhalgarh Kelwara till 1615 when peace was signed with Jahangir[85] with capital at Chavand Pratap, free from agression in 1575-1597 A.D., died in 1597 A.D.

and expeditious to Mewar were given up some time by Akbar and never seriouslly taken up till the time of Jahangir.[86]

As per the submission terms conceded to Maharana Amar Singh, in lieu of the *mansab* conferred on Kanwar Karan Singh and the military services to be rendered to the Mughal State, the *Kanwar* was confirmed in the *watan jagir* of *pargana* Udaipur besides assignment of revenues of various other *parganas* from *Sarkar* Chittor (erstwhile Mewar Principality) and some *parganas* of *Sarkar* Sirohi and a few *parganas* from *Subahas* of Ujjain and Malwa in *tankhwa jagir*. The other *parganas* of south Chittor not assigned to the *Kanwar* remained in the directly administered Mughal territory, in *Khalsa* or assignable to any other *Jagirdar*.[87] The *parganas* assigned in *tankhwa jagir* were transferable to *Khalsa* or could be assigned to any other person. In the time of Raja Raj Singh I, Shahjahan converted many of the *parganas* in *tankhwa jagir* into Mughal territory—increased and decreased sometimes namely[88] *Pargana* Jodhpur, Mandal, Ghairabad, Mandalgarh, Jahazpur, Sawar, Phalia, Brurara, Hurrah, Badnor, etc. but later on Aurangzeb, after his success in war of succession, reassigned a few of these.[89] Again, in lieu of the *jazya*, the *parganas* of Pur Mandal, Badnor and Mandalgarh were converted into *Khalsa*.[90] The Rana had taken these *Parganas* on *Ijara* and later occupied them but was obliged to surrender to the Royal order. Letter of Wazir Asad Khan to Maharana Amar Singh[91] forbids Rana from any future interference in *Khalsa* administration of these *parganas* and required him to send a stamped written bond to the effect.[92] The letter of Nawab Jummatud Mulk Asad Khan to Wazir Bakshi ul Nawab Baharmaud Khan clearly mentions the Raja as the *Jagirdar*[93] for having accepted all the terms.[94] They were returned to the Rana on the condition of paying Rs. 1 Lac per year to the Royal treasury. As the Rana never paid full amount, they were again escheated to *Khalsa* administration.[95]

Dungarpur, Banswara & Sirohi

Dungarpur

Though included in the *Ain* as a part of Sarkar Sirohi, in the pre-Mughal period, Dungarpur formed a part of *Subah* Gujrat and even during the Mughal age, it was subject to the administration of Governor of Gujrat. During the Gujrat Sultanate, it was constituted as a full *Sarkar*. The Chief of Duangarpur, Rawal Sahis Mal, owed a contigent of 1000 *sawars* in lieu of *watan jagir* whereas the other territory of the *Zimmidari* was assignable to other *jagirdars*.[96] The *Zimmidar* was exempted from the payment of *peshkash*.[97] In earlier times, the Duangarpur chief had also owed allegiance to Rana of Mewar. Sahis Mal submitted to Raja Todar Mal and was awarded a *mansab* of 2500.[98] However, despite the political changes, this claim was never surrendered. The Dungar chiefs, Rawal Punja, Rawal Girdhar, Rawal Jaswant Singh, Rawal Ghuman Singh and Rawal Ram Singh owed allegiance and military service to the Mughals.[99] In Aurangzeb's time, Rawal Rana Singh held a mansab of 1000 *zats* and *sawars*.

Banswara

The *Zimmidari* of Banswara also constituted a part of the Sultanate of Gujrat[100] though the Mewar chiefs never surrendered their claim for exacting allegiance. Rawal Udhai Singh had fought for Rana Sanga against Babur and died at Bayana.[101] Uggar Sain accepted Akbar's supremacy and his successor Udahai Bhan, Sammar Singh, Kushal Singh, Ajab Singh, Bhim Singh and Bishen Singh continued to owe allegiance.[102] At times, the Mewar chiefs favourably tried to exact allegiance at accession to *Gadi* and for failure in this ceremony, Rana Jagat singh and Udhai Singh sent forces.[103] Raj Singh sent Fateh Chand Kaishi (1659 A.D.) who exacted 1 Lac Rs. as damages and 10 villages and 1 elephant as *nazarana* for Mewar Chiefs.[104]

Sirohi

The *Zimmidari* of Sirohi was a part of the Gujrat Sultanate as one of the *Sarkars*[105] and had also owed allegiance to Udhaipur[106]; paid tribute to the Diwan—*Subah* of Gujrat.[107] The *Zimmidar* of Sirohi, Sultan Singh submitted to Raja Todar Mal and accepted Mughal supremacy. He undertook to serve with 2000 sawars. The Governor of Gujrat[108] also presented Rs. 50000, 100 *Ashrfies* as *peshkash*. In return, he was presented with a robe of honour jewel for the turban and an elephant.[109] Successors remained faithful but from the time of Akbar to the Viceroyalty of Prince Dara Shikoh (Shah Jahan's reign), the *Zimmidar* never attended with forces.[110] The Mewar Chiefs devastated the territory in the reigns of Jagat Singh and Raj Singh for exacting allegiance.[111]

Partap Garh (Devlia)

Tej Singh, *Zimmidar* of Devlia (Partap Garh), descendant from the Mewar family accepted Akbar's authority. His successors continued to accept the Mughal supremacy. All the same, the Mewar chiefs continued to claim allegiance from them. Rana Jagat Singh sent his force against Devlia but when Hari Singh was awarded *mansab* by Shah Jahan, the forces of Jagat Singh withdrew. Raj Singh again sent forces and got allegiance.[112]

Zimmidars and the Jagir System

Though Tod and other writers on the Rajasthan history have given a comprehensive account of the political and military aspects[113], they have not gone deeper into the concept of administrative relationship between the Mughal State and the Rajput principalities. Consequently, for the period under discussion, they have not been able to analyse the agrarian setup of the *Zimmidari* lands.[114] Now with the Rajasthan Archives for historical research at hand, a clear picture of the land administration in the principalities of Rajasthan during the Mughal age can be constructed and many a fact of the *Ain* regarded as riddle hitherto become self-explanatory.

The relationship between the Mughal State and the Rajput *Zimmidaries* was based on four-fold aspects. (1) Submission was followed by the confirmation of the loyal *Zimmidars* in their *Zimmidari* and the enrollment of the *Zimmidars* amongst the Mughal nobility ; (ii) the prerogative of the Mughal government to regulate the succession to the '*Gadi*' in a *Zimmidari*; (iii)confirmation in the *Zimmidari* meant the grant of *watan jagir* only.—The other *jagir* lands, if awarded, depended on the *mansab* of the *Zimmidar* and the discretion of the Mughal monarch; (iv) internal autonomy of the *Zimmidar* within the territorial limits of the *watan jagir*.

Regulation of Succession to Gadi

The fact of the submission and confirmation of the Rajput chiefs and their enrollment amongst the Mughal nobility has already been described. As regards the succession problem, every Rajput principality was governed by the law of heredity and barring Jodhpur, even by the practice of *primo geniture.*[115] Rana Gaj Singh during his life time had made a request to Shahjahan that he should be succeeded by his son. He accepted the request and recognised Maharaja Jaswant Singh (1) and awarded *mansab* of 4000 *zat & sawar*. The author of Vir Vinod comments that the practice of deviation from the *primo geniture* and accession being hereditary did not exist anywhere else except amongst the Rathors. But every succession to a Raj '*Gadi*' (miniature throne) of a *Zimmidari* was subject to the approval of the Mughal Government which was regarded as confirmed formally only when the latter presented *Tikka* (for the ceremony of the embalment of the forehead) along with a *Farman* of recognition of the new Chief.

However, at times, guided by either personal favouritism based on the meritorious services rendered by the Prince or his capability for future service, the Mughal monarch set aside the *primo geniture* or even hereditary claims of the prospective Chief and asserted his personal choice for installation on the '*Gadi*'. Such a royal prerogative is clear from Jahangir's assertion in his Memoirs at the vacancy of '*Gadi*' of Amber in

1614 A.D. After the death of Raja ManSingh. Jahangir comments, "After the death of Man Singh, I sent for his son Mirza Bhao Singh. According to Hindu practice, the rightful claimant to the *Zimmidari Gadi* was Maha Singh, son of Jagat Singh (the eldest of the late Raja Man Singh who had died in the latter's life-time) but I did not approve of it. I selected Bhao Singh and awarded him the title of Mirza Raja and the *mansab* of 4000 & 3000 *sawar* to succeed the *Gadi* of his ancestors. In order to please Maha Singh, I added a *mansab* of 500 to his previous *mansab*..."[116] The claim was invariably exercised by the Mughal monarchs. Akbar had set aside the claim of K. Duddha, son of late Raja Surjan to the *Gaddi* of Boondi and installed his younger brother K. Bhoj as the *Rana*.[117] Jahangir also asserted his choice for Dalpat Singh's succession to Rao Rai Singh at the *Gadi* of Bikaner in preference to the wishes of the deceased for his younger son, K. Suraj Singh.[118] Aurangzeb installed Anup singh on the *Gadi* of Bikaner within the lifetime of Raja Karan Singh, the latter's father and the ruling chief, Raja Karan Singh, who had not helped Aurangzeb during the war of succession to the Mughal throne.[119] After the death fo Raja Jaswant Singh of Jodhpur (1678 A.D.), Aurangzeb' recognition of Inder Singh, 'a royal grandee' to the *Gaddi* in preference to the hereditary claim of Ajit Singh, the posthumous son of the deceased Chief and later on the conversion of the principality into *Khalsa* land is a well-known fact in the annals of Marwar.[120] Howsoever politically inexpedient and inopportune it was,[121] Aurangzeb's assertion of royal prerogative based on the past precedents is untenable.

Under Akbar, after the conquest, the Rajasthan principalities were incorporated in *Subah* Ajmer which was divided into seven Sarkars, viz. Ajmer, Chittor, Ranthambor, Jodhpur, Sirohi Nagar and Bikaner.[122] On geographical and tribal basis, the *Subah* consisted of three divisions: Mewar comprising the Sisodia Rajputs in the entire Sarkar of Chittor, Marwar with Rathore Rajputs in the Sarkars of Ajmer, Jodhpur, Sirohi, Nagor and Bikaner, Hadaotri with the Hada (Hara) Rajputs in the Sarkar of Nagor.[123] However, any other portion of the *Zimmidar*, if not assigned to him as *tankhwa jagirs* could be declared either as *khalsa* or assigned to any other ordinary *Jagirdar*.[124] Thus the extent of the ordinary *jagir* lands attached to the *watan jagir* of a *Zimmidar* varied within the same family from time to time depending both on the nature of the services rendered by the *Zimmidars* and the discretion of the monarch.[125] It was always the considered policy of a Princely *Zimmidar* to get the *jagir* lands adjacent to his *watan jagir* so as to form a composite block comprising, if possible, his pre-Mughal principality. As the ordinary *jagir land* (in lieu of salary) lapsed with the death of a ruling Prince and reverted to Mughal *Paibaqi* or *Khalsa*, the succeeding Chief had to make fresh endeavours for the *de-*

novo grant of these *jagirs* which was again conditioned by the *mansab* awarded and the services rendered by the new Chief.[126] At times, all the *tankhwa jagirs* held previously by the family were not restored though conversely a Chief could own much larger extent of *jagirs* than ever held previously by his family. (instances from Amber, Udaipur, Jaisalmer). Still, at times, if the grant of a *tankhwa jagir* did not fully cover the area of the pre-Mughal family *Zimmidari*, an ambitious Chief would like to make up the gap by taking the remaining territory on *ijara* from either the official assignee or directly from *khalsa* administration.[127] Mostly, the principalities lost a substantial portion of their pre-Mughal territories which henceforth were directly administered as Mughal territory, whether in *Khalsa* or assignable to any *Jagirdar*. Even as such, a *Zimmidar* was confirmed only in his *watan-jagir* and regarded as hereditary whereas the other portion of the *Zimmidari* was conferred on him as *jagir* in lieu of the services rendered to the Mughal State. Apart from this, he could lay claim only to the *watan jagir*.[128]

Land Revenue Administration

As regards revenue administration, the *Zimmidaries* of Amber (*Sarkar* Ajmer) Bundi, Kotah (*Sarkar* Ranthambhor) were declared *amli.*[129] For Ajmer, *Ain* declares all the 28 *parganas amli* with measurement figures and assessed revenues for each *Pargana*. In South Ranthambhor, out of 73 *mahals*, 55 *mahals* are declared *amli*, bearing measurment figures and assessed revenues while 18 *mahals* are *ghair amli* for which no measurment figures are recorded and the revenues are declared *naqdi*, i.e. fixed unassessed amounts.[130] The major portions of Mewar (S. Chittor) were declared *amli* while the *Pargana* of Udaipur proper with few others were *Ghair amli.*[131] In contrast to the repeated assertion of independence, such is the irony of agrarian history of Mewar that unlike the *Zimmidaries* of Jodhpur or Bikaner or Sirohi, etc., its major portions were declared *amli*, surveyed and assessed in accordance with the Mughal practice.[132]

Most of the *Zimmidaries* included in S. Nagar were declared *amli.*[133] The *Zimmidari* of Jodhpur remained *Ghair amli* till its annexation to the Mughal State in 1678.[134] It mentions the appointment of the *Qanungos* in Jodhpur for the first time for the preparation of the *Taqsim* and the '*jama*' documents, the translation of the Hindi documents in Persian. It also notes the appointment of Shri Mohd. Anwar as *Amin*, Abul Wasim Shivaji as *Karori* and Ganga Ram as the chief *Qanungo* for the accomplishment of the task of assessment and realisation of revenue. The *Zimmidaries* of Bikaner, Jaisalmer (South Bikaner)[135] and Banswarh, Dungurpur, Sirohi and Jalor (South Sirohi)[136] remained *Ghair amli.*[137]

The chief *Zimmidars* undoubtedly enjoyed the privilege of making further assignment for military and charitable purposes.[138] Ordinarily, the Mughal Government did not make any *Madad-i-Maash* grant in the land of a Chief *Zimmidar* ever in *Watan Payana.*[139] For typical *Zimmidari* of Jodhpur, Bikaner, Sirohi, Baiswanah, Durgapur, Jalor, *Ain* does not quote any *Surghal* assignments.

For *Watan Parganas* of any of the Rajasthan *Zimmidaries* mentioned before, no *Surghal* can be traced in *Ain.* But if any portion or the entire *Zimmidari* was incorporated in *Khalsa* administration, the Mughal Government had the right to make grants of *Madad-i-Maash* therein.[140]

Footnotes

1. Not within my scope to discuss the political and military history of these chiefs before conquest or submission.
2. Fall of Chittor, Haldigahat references in *Akbar-Nama,* Beveridge, I, 117.
3. Vide original treaty *Vir Vinod*; Tod, II, 428.
4. *A.N.* II, 15. Tod II, 286. Amber had been a dependency of Ajmer. M.U. Tr. I, p. 409—the latter being a district of Maldeo's kingdom prior to the Mughal conquest.
5. *Ain,* I, p. 508; A.N. ii, 155.
6. *Jahangir Memoirs*—4000 *zat* and 3000 *sawar*.
7. *Vir Vinod*, 1289, M.U. 5000 *zat* 5000 *sawar*. Tod, 287, 6000 *mansab*.
8. Tod, 288.
9. Bishen Singh M.U. 3000 *Sawar*, Jai Singh (Aurangzeb's reign).
10. *Vir Vinod*, pp. 1276-1298; Tod, pp. 279-289.
11. Dr. Saran, p. 147, wrongly thinks that Jaisalmer was not a part of *Subah* Ajmer. See *Ain*, II, p. 282.
12. *Vir Vinod*, p. 814.
13. *Moota Raja.*
14. *Vir Vinod*, p. 845.
15. T.A. August 26 *Rajab* 99 A.H. *Vir Vinod*, 815 II, 444 with 1500 *rank.*
16. 1000 *Zat & Sawar*, *Vir Vinod*, p. 815.
17. *Raiputana Gazette*, III A., p. 59 *mansab* 4000-5000.
18. 3000, 2000 with a standard and title of Raja (Jahangir Shahjahan, *Rajputana Gazetteer*, Vol. III. A, p. 59 that he held the rank of 4000, later 5000.
19. Shahjahn & Aurangzeb, 4000, *Zat & Sawar*, *Vir Vinod*, p. 821.
20. Inder Singh of Nagor—for management—later on set aside.
21. *Vir Vinod*, pp. 829-312; total 814-834; Tod 23-55.
22. *M.I.*, p. 171.
23. M.I., p. 21.
24. West Ajmer and other sources.
25. *Vir Vinod*, p. 833; Ajit Singh occupied Jodhpur on March 3, 1707 A.D. after Aurangzeb's death—Bahadur Shah recognised him as the Maharaja of Jodhpur, *Vir Vinod*, pp. 833-34.
26. *M.I.*, p. 17.
27. *M.I.*, pp. 21-22—total imcome, Rs. 2,55,000.

28. *M.I.*, p. 17.
29. *Ain*, ii, p. 281.
30. *Jahangir Farman*, dated 21st May 1615 A.D. vide *Vir Vinod*, pp. 239-49.
31. *T.A.* II, 229-230; Elliot, V., pp. 335-336.
32. *Mansab* of 400 in 1605—raised to 5000 by Jahangir.
33. *Vir Vinod*, p. 488.
34. *Vir Vinod*, p. 489
35. *Vir Vinod*, p. 493.
36. *Vir Vinod*, p. 498.
37. Ibid.
38. *Ain.*, I., 477. Blochmann and other chronicles are silent when the chief accepted Akbar's supremacy .
39. *Ibid.*, R & B, 33-34.
40. Tod-II, pp. 209-211.
41. Dr. Saran, p. 147, wrongly thinks that Jaisalmer was not a part of *Subah* Ajmer. See *Ain*, II, p. 282.
42. Tod, II, pp. 209-10.
43. *Ibid.*, p. 210.
44. Dr. Saran, p. 147, is not correct that the status of Jaiselmer was different from Amber, Bikaner and Jodhpur—Tod, p. 218 is right in thinking that Jaisalmer had been shelved of the major portion of its pre-Mughal territories but this had been the case with every other *Zimmidari* excepting that other Chiefs were more fortunate to hold higher *mansabs* and larger *tankhwa jagirs* in lieu thereof.
45. *Vir Vinod*, p. 84.
46. *A.N.*, II, tr. Bev. 494-95; *Vir Vinod*, pp. 84-85.
47. *Vir Vinod*, 85; Tod—II, 382-83.
48. Tod, p. 384.
49. *Mansab* 2000 *zat* and *sawar*, *Vir Vinod*, 109-11.
50. *Ain*, I, Blockman, p. 409.
51. *Vir Vinod*, p. 111.
52. *Vir Vinod*, p. 111. Dated A.H. 1016.
53. Tod, p. 387.
54. Tod, pp. 389-90.
55. Tod II, pp. 390-91; *Vir Vinod*, pp. 111-113.

56. See Tod, p. 442.

57. *Vir Vinod*, p. 112, p. 1407 from *Badshahnama*; Lahori Vol. I, p. 401.

58. Dr. Saran, p. 141—not correct in statement that Jahangir created Kota State through *Altamgha* grant—it was created by Shahjahan, dated 1041 A.H. 1631 A.D.

59. *Vir Vinod*, pp. 1409-10; M.U.

60. *Vir Vinod*, 1411.

61. *Vir Vinod*, p. 493.

62. *Vir Vinod*, p. 112, 1407 A.D.; Lahori, Vol. I, p. 401.

63. (refer to some of the negotiations for attending personally-Dr. A.R. Srivastava, I. H. C.)

64. Tod, I, 239. Vide Ms. *Amarkavya Vanshavali,* folio 48 (a) Ms. *Sisod Vanshavali,* fol. 29 (a) & (b).

65. Sarkar, *Later Mughals,* p. 43; *Vir Vinod*, pp. 239—249.

66. *Vir Vinod*, p. 312.

67. Tod, I, pp. 296-297.

68. *Vir Vinod*, pp. 319-322. Also Sharma, p. 148.

69. Lahori, Persian text, Vol. III, pp. 370-71.

70. *Ibid.*, p. 345; Sharma, p. 149.

71. *Vir Vinod*, p. 342.

72. *Vir Vinod*, p. 338.

73. *Vir Vinod*, p. 402.

74. *Vir Vinod*, vide *Aurangzeb's Nishan*, Sharma, pp. 157-58.

75. Rana's Letter, Tod, I, pp. 302-3.

76. Sharma, pp. 169-172.

77. Sharma, p. 173.

78. Sharma, p. 176.

79. Sharma, p. 180; *Vir Vinod*, p. original *Farman*, 651-652.

80. Reply in *Farman*; original *Farman* with Raghvbir Singh, dated 18th July 1681.—relations cordial till 1698—Jai Singh's death.

81. *Vir Vinod*, p. 730.

82. Tod, I, p. 314.

83. *Vir Vinod*, p. 730.

84. *Ain*, I, pp. 278-79; *A.N.* Persian Text II., pp. 408-09; *Tabqat-i-Akbari*, Persian text, p. 284; Badaoni, Persian text, Vol. II, 105. In February 1568, Chittor put under Asaf Khan.

85. Sharma, p. 91.—even after Haldi Ghat—increasing his hold in Central Mewar, p. 107—Sharma has worked on some copper plates v.s. 1633—grant of land to Balbhadra—no. 26/133, *jagir* 96, C.O.; Gobunda occupied by Akbar in 1576- Badaoni, Persian text II, p. 240; *A.N.* III 164-65; occupied north-east corner of Western mountain chain to the southeast point up to Udaipur—1576-77; Udaipur with Bhagwan Das-*A.N* Persian text III, p. 169; Khilwara occupied by the Mughals in 1578 A.D. *A.N.* –Persian text III, pp. 204-205—Mughal masters over fight in Kumbalgarh over major portions—Rana in Dholan in Kumbhalgarh—1579-80-Mughal Supremacy in the central region of the territory and the Rana in his hilly homes—*A.N* III, Persian text, p. 229. Tod has gone to the extent (Vol. I, p. 398) that Pratap wandered and virtually stawed but rebuilt, Jha, *Udaipur Ka Ithas.*, pp. 455-457, Sharma, 114—Maharana in the hilly tracts of Dholan—Rana success in Magra against Rathors V.S. 1585 A.D.—*Jagir Misal* no. 1722/93; Sharma, 116. By 1585 A.D., with the help of K. Amar Singh, he occupied the major portions of northeast of Mewar with Udaipur, Mohi, Gogunda, Manda, Pandwara as the chief places. (*Vir Vinod*, pp. 163—164—occupied 36 places; Plate no. 368 c.o.u. Sharma, p. 117).

86. Amar Singh, prince of Kumphalgarh (1597 A.D.) Chittor and Mawalgarh areas under Mughals—(Ontala, Nohi, Bagore, Maudal, Mandalgarh, Chittor and several other places with Mughals when Prince Salim came in 1599 A.D. *A.N.* III, Persian 819 Beni Prashad—*Jahangir*, p. 226—prolonged war under Jahangir till peace in 1615).

87. Vide *Farman*, *Ain*, I, 508.

88. *Vir Vinod*, p. 414.

89. Badnor, Mandalgarh, Giaspur, Basawar, etc. V.S. *Vir Vinod*, p. 434, vide Aurangzeb's *Farman*.

90. *Vir Vinod*, p. 730.

91. *Vir Vinod*, p. 737

92. *Vir Vinod*, p. 740.

93. *Vir Vinod*, p. 734.

94. These *Parganas* were later assigned by the Mughal government to Karan Singh and Jaggar Singh, *Vir Vinod*, p. 740—Later in a revenue of one *karor Dam Jamma* of *Pargana* Sirohi and *Pargana* Alamgarh assigned to Rana Amar Singh in lieu of service with 1000 *sawars* in Deccan vide *Yaddasht of Amiul Umara Shaista Khan*, 7th *Zilkat* 1114 A.H. / 1703 A.D. 26th March, *Vir Vinod*, p. 749.

95. *Vir Vinod*, pp. 75-51.

96. In the Sultanate period was assigned to Fateh Khan, Rustam Khan Balochan, etc., *Mirat*, I.

97. *Ibid.*

98. *M.I.*, p. 136.

99. *Vir Vinod*, pp. 1007-08.

100. *M.I.*, 17.

101. *Vir Vinod*, p. 1031.

102. *Vir Vinod*, pp. 1031-33.

103. *Ibid.*, 1033,319-22, 434-35.

104. *Vir Vinod*, pp. 434-35.

105. *M.I.*, 17.

106. *Vir Vinod*, p. 1097—a Parish dated 983 A.H./1575, Man Singh asvassal of Mewar chiefs.

107. *M.I.*, p. 24.

108. *M.I.*, 134 also presented Rs. 50,000, 100 *Ashrfies* as *Peshkash*.

109. *M.S.*, tr. 190-91.

110. *M.S.*, Ibid.

111. *Vir Vinod*, pp. 1099-1101.

112. *Vir Vinod*, pp. 1061.

113. Tod; Ohja, *Vir Vinod*, Sharma and a few others.

114. Tod's imagination was circumscribed by to much of reliance on the local annals of the principalities. The later Indian writers followed first through Kavira Shyman Das, the author has extensively quoted the original documents for the Udaipur Darbar of his own; he has not been able to understand the technical nature of the land administration quite evident from the narated documents.

115. *Vir Vinod*, p. 821.

116. *Vir Vinod*, p. 1286, accession on 9th *Jamaidi-ul Sani* 1023 A.H./16th Jully 1614 A.D.

117. *Vir Vinod*, p. 108; Tod ii.p. 261.

118. *Tuzk*, p. 108.

119. *Vir Vinod*, p. 498.

120. *Waqai Ajmer*—pp. 74, 80-84, 114, 167, 241-46; *Maasir-i-Alamgiri*, pp. 172, 175-76; *Nuskha's Dislkusha*, folio 76[a]; *Mirat*, I, p. 277; *Vir Vinod*, pp. 829-33; also M. Ather Ali, 'The Causes of the Rathor Rebellion of 1679; *I.H.C.* Session, Delhi, 1961.

121. *Ibid.*; see details in Sarkar—*Aurangzeb*, III, pp. 369-(?).

122. *Ain*, J. II, pp. 278-282.

123. *Ibid.*, pp. 271-277.

124. Quite clear from the R.A. Jaipur of the Ajmer rulers.

125. See vast changes in the *Jagir* shifts with the Amber Chiefs. Even within the lifetime of one princely *Zimmidar*, his *Jagirs* varied from time to time.

126. Instances from Amber for Shahjahan and Aurangzeb.

127. *Ijara* instances from Amber, Udaipur Records, Jai Singh, II; *Vir Vinod.*

128. *Waqai Ajmer*—Jodhpur case.

129. *Ain*, ii, pp. 278-280.

130. *Ibid.*, R.A.J. record the assessment done on the Mughal lines for these areas.

131. *Ibid.*, pp. 278-79.

132. This was bound to happen in face of the recalcitrants of the Chiefs in Akbar's reign as it led to the annexation of the *Zimmidari* areas to the Mughal State. In accordance with the Mughal practice, any *Zimmidari* area attached to the Mughal territories was immediately surveyed and assessed by the Mughal revenue officials. (see B.G. tr. Bhor, pp 72) *Waqai Rathambhor* explains the same procedure after the annexation of Marwar in 1678 A.D. in Aurangzeb's reign. Dr. Sharma (p.142) is wrong in his statement that Rana Karan Singh divided his territories into *Paiamas* etc. They had already been so divided during the period of Mughal occupation as is clear from Shah Jahan's *Farman* of 1615 A.D. to Rana Amar Singh and Karan Singh (Sharma, p. 142)—concerning the division already done by the Mughals. Survey and assessment were essentially on Mughal lines is clear from Tod's *Annals* (Vol. I, pp. 397-8). *Ain* (i. pp. 278-79) mentions the survey of Chittor with 26 *Paimas*, 8 *Ghair amli*, 18 *amli* with 1,678, 8000 *Bighas*, 17 *Biswas*, total revenues for all the 26 Parganas, 30, 047, 649 *Dams*. (*f.n.* equallly wrong in his statement that the realisation of State demand was based on the principle laid down in *Dharm Shastras*. For this, he quotes Jagat Singh Kavya, 51. Such a source is not authentic as it is only of general family praise account. The revenue system had been bought in accordance with the Mughal practice. Vide *Farman*, V.V. pp. 269-71 is clearly wrong.

133. *Ain*, 281-282.29 *amli*—2 *Ghairamli*.

134. *Waqai*, Rajasthan, pp. 163-173 explains in detail the survey and the measurement operation carried on by the Mughal officials in Jodhpur *Parganas*.

135. *Ain*, pp. 281-82.

136. *Ain*, p. 281.

137. For these, *Ain* does not record the measurment tables.

138. Raja Raj Singh made the grant of Bhawali in P. Mandal to Bhan (Also Sharma, p. 123 copper plate Ins. No. 419—dated 9th of dark half of Asad, V.S. 1729 (1662 A.D.) and a *jagir* of village Kalyan in Jahazpur in V.S. 1715 (1658

A.D.) vide Photograph no. 26/10 B. *Jagir* (Also, V.V. II. Pp. 453-54 quotes the grant of *jagirs* of Parsohi to Kesri Singh and Salumber to Rattan Singh respectively. Ram Singh and Bhima were granted Sakrod and Ragheda (*girwa*) respectively as rent-free lands. (Photograph, Patta no. 26/10 B. *jagir* A.S. 95 of Commissioner's office of 15th of bright half of *Jaislha*, V.S. 1734/- and 8th of dark half of *Kartika*, V.S. 1734 respectively.

139. *Ain*, I, pp. 281-282.

140. After the occupation of Hurda Shahpura and Badnor, Akbar granted the villages of Kayaa, Katdi, Arneta and Kanya from these Mahals on 23rd *Ramzan* H 982/1575 A.D. for *Dargha Sharif*, Ajmer, vide File no. 20/11, *Samvat* 93 in Commissioner's office Udaipur; Also see Akbar's Original *Farman* (*Dharga Sharif Ajmer*) dated 23rd *Shah Ramzan* 972H/1567 A.D. makes *waqf* grant for a few villages in South Chittor. These grants have continued throughout till recent times.)

6

Zamindars of the Central Hilly Region in *Subah* Malwa

The entire *Subah* of Malwa was subjected to the Mughal rule in Akbar's reign. Of the chief *Zimmidars*, Raja Madhukar Bundela was reduced to submission by Akbar in 1578 A.D.[1] Though helped by the geographical features of mountaineous character and deep ravines, at times, the Bundela chief still showed recalcitrance.[2] He was confirmed in his territory as *Jagirdar*. Later on, his son Bir Singh Bundela was faithful to Jahangir and his son Jujhar Singh was enrolled by Shahjahan as a regular *Mansabdar* of 4000 *zat* and *sawar* in 1628 A.D. Afterwards, because of recalcitrant behaviors, he was degraded in *mansab* and deprived of a part of his *jagir*.[3] This further led to his complete destruction in 1634 A.D. and the territories of Datia, Jhansi and other forts of Bundel Khand were attached to the Mughal administration.[4]

Another Chief *Zimmidar*, Raja Ram Chand Baghel of Bhatta submitted to Akbar in 1584 A.D. and his son was held as hostage at the Mughal Court.[5] His son, Bir Bhadra, rebelled in 1598 A.D. but was reduced to submission.[6] The chiefs of Bhutta were confined in their territory as *Jagirdars* and rendered meritiorious military services for the Mughal State.[7] The Chiefs of Bundela and Bhatta were governed by the same *Zimmidari* regulations as the Rajasthan Chiefs for the grant of *Jagirs* and the military obligations.[8]

The *Zimmidari* of Rampura, though historically associated with Rajashtan and Gujrat, was put under the administration of *Subha* Malwa.[9] Rao Durga Bhan of Rajpura Submitted to Akbar in 1583 A.D. and was enrolled as the Mughal *Mansabdar*[10] and was confirmed in his *Zimmidari* as *Jagirdar*. He served Akbar and Jahangir for nearly 40 years. In the 40th year of Akbar's reign, he held the *mansab* of 1500 and Jahangir in Tuzk[11] comments that before entering the Mughal service, the Rao was under Udai Singh of Mewar and that he served his father and him for 40 years and reached the rank of 4000 *mansab*. In Aurangzeb's reign, Rao Gopal Singh, the *Zimmidar* of Rampur, held a personal *jagir* and also paid *peshkash* to *Subah* Malwa.[12] It seems that Rao Gopal Singh did not hold any *mansab* under Aurangzeb.

Later on, his son Rattan Singh embraced Islam and was appointed the *Zimmidar* of Rampura, renamed as Islampura, on the removal of his father. He was granted the title of Raja Islam Khan with a *mansab* of 1500 *zat* & 1000 *sawar*.[13]

Footnotes

1. Raja of Bundela defeated in 1578 A.D. vide *A.N.* III, pp. 209-210, 229-231 & 261.

2. Prince Murad, the *subahdar* of Malwa complained against the chief for not having come for personal submission and the latter was ordered to make obedience. Vide *A.N.* III, pp. 604-606; Tr. III, pp. 900-924.

3. Vide *Ain* I, p. 203. M.U. II, p. 215 given only 2000 *Z* & *S* and rent to Deccan Campaign.

4. *Ain* II, p. 106.

5. *A.N.* III, p. 420.

6. *Ibid.*, III, p. 728.

7. In 1634, Amar Singh, the ruler of Bandhir helped Abdullah Khan Firoz Jang in suppressing the rebellious *Zammindar* of Tatanpur in Bihar (vide *Ain,* I, Part II, pp. 74-76).

8. vide P.G., p. 124. Dr. Saran is entirely wrong in his statement that the Chiefs of Bundela and Bhatta, unlike Rajasthan Chiefs, were never fully subjected to the Mughal authority and that the services of Chief of Bhatta to Abdullah Khan was voluntary rather than fulfillment of any stipulated obligation. For want of the original Mughal *farmans* and documents in connection with these *Zammidars*, it is not possible to work out the details of the *Jagir* system as is posible to analyze in case of Rajasthan *Zamindaris*. The general statements in the *Chronicles* are alike for all types of *Zamindaries* and there is no reason to suppose that the pattern of *Jagirs* was different in Malwa.

9. *Ain,* I, II, p. 249, in its geographical description of *Subah* Gujrat includes *Pargana* Rampura in Gujrat but the original revenue documents put it under the administration of *Subahdar* of Malwa.

10. *A.N.* iii, p. 423

11. *Tuzk-i-Jahangiri*, I, p. 283.

12. (See ref. R.A., category 3, Reg. No. 226. Gopal Singh, the *Zimmidar* of Rampura held the entire *Zimmidari* in *Jagir* and paid *Peshkash.*

13. RA *Akhbarat* 29th *Shawal* regnal year 44/8th April, 1700 A.D. The news related that Rattan Singh, son of Rao Gopal Singh, *Zimmidar* of Rampura alias Islampur approached of his own Mukhatar Khan, the *Subahadar* of Malwa, who reconfirmed his case for the grant of *Zimmidari* vide removal of his father which was accepted by the Emperor. Such of the other cases are also on record. R.A. *Akhbarat*, dated 9th of *Shabban* of the regnal year of Aurangzeb states that Nil Kanth and three other persons (who were the *Zimmidars* of *Subah* Malwa) embraced Islam of their own free will and were confirmed in their *Zimmidaries*.

7

The Zamindars in Malwa

Some of the Rajasthan Archives of Aurangzeb's reign dealing with the *Zimmidaries* of *Subah* Malwas bring out their main feathures.[1] Each of the *Zimmidaries* is shown with its revenues regularly assessed by the *Amin*[2] and majority of the *Zimmidars* are *amli*.[3] Some of the *Zimmidari* revenues (*peshkash*) were assigned to the Mughal State *Jagirdars*. As such, *Zimmidaries* also bear the name of the assignee while in other cases, the *Zimmidars* were required to pay the *peshkash muqari* (revenues) directly to the Mughal State. For some *Zimmidaries*, the revenues for payment in *peshkash* and personal *jagir* of the *Zimmidar* are shown. A few of the *Zimmidars* are stated to be docile and regular in payment of *peshkash* while others are shown as '*Zur talb*" who would pay only when forced by the contingent of the *Faujdar* or *Jagirdar*.

Footnotes

1. R.A. Yaddasht- *'Haquqat-i-Zimmidaran Mutilqa Subah Malwa'*. Cataloging No. 3, Reg. Nos. 228, 229, 300. They are undated but the names of the important assignees can be traced amongst the nobles of Aurangzeb. For example, (Zainal Abideen as *Jagirdar* of the *Zimmidar* of Bans balla and Deolia and Rampura in Abdeen was the *Diwan* of *Subah* Khandesh.

2. *Ibid.*, Regd nos. 229 & 300 quote numerous *Zimmidaries* in the *Paragnas* assessed by the *Amin* named Mir Hamaid.

3. The availability of the area figures in the *Ain* of the Indian *Paraganas* of Ratlam, Badhnawar (*Ain* II, p. 209); Deola (*Ibid.*, p. 216) clearly indicate that the assessment was based on regular measurement and a record of rights. As most of the *Zimmadaries* form a part of *Pargana* only, it is not possible to trace in the names of the *Tappah* and the *Mauza Zimmadaries* in the *Ain.* Moreover, because of the variation in the texts of the *Ain,* many of the *Pargana* names cannot be identified. Above all, a *Pargana* without measurment figures in the *Ain* would not remain so throughout in the Mughal age as the process of consolidation and measurement recorded many a *Ghair amli Paragna* of Akbar's reign into *amli Parganas* in the later reigns under the Mughals.

8

The Zamindars of Sub-Himalayan Ranges of Kumaon

Like the Punjab Hills, the Chiefs of the Kumaon Hills also were subjected to the Mughal *Zimmidari* regulations and were attached for administrative control to the *Faujdar* of Bareli. In 1587, the Raja of Kumaon came to Delhi for personal submission.[1] In 26th year (A.D.), a revolt on the part of hill chieftains, Ram Shah of Kumaon, Mukat Sen, Ram Karan and many others was suppressed[2] which shows that they had been formally reduced much earlier in Akbar's reign. Jahangir mentions the Raja of Kumaon as a faithful *Zimmidar* and bestowed on him his territory in *jagir*.[3] Though in Shajahan's reign, a revolt on the part of the Chief was suppressed again by Khalilullah Khan in 1654 A.D.,[4] *Ain* incorporates all the *Zimmidaries* of the Kumaon Hills in the 21 *Mahals* of *Sarkar* Kumaon, *Subah* Delhi, out of which revenues for only 12 *Mahals* are recorded while the area tables are not available for any of the *Mahals*. As such, all the *Zimmidaries* in these hills were *ghair amli* with even indeterminate revenues for few of them.[5] For the purposes of maintenance of control and revenue administration, Hill chieftains were subject to the administration of *Subah* Delhi though the *Faujdari* division located at Bahili and did not have enough direct dealing with the Central Government as thought by Dr. Saran.[6] Dr. Saran's analysis[7] is entirely wrong. His statements that the chiefs had diplomatic relations with the Empire before and after subjection and that the figures represent the levy and stipulated figures to be paid by the Chiefs, which was never enforced, are baseless. The revenue figures are the respective revenues of the *Mahals* from which the Chiefs were assigned personal *jagirs* and others could be given in *jagir* to the Mughal S tate officials. The contingent figures of 3,000 cavalry and 450 infantry stand time for all the chieftains of the Kumaon Hills and even not including the *dasturmul* and as no *zabti* system was enforced.

Footnotes

1. *A.N.* III, p. 353; Bad. II, pp. 365-66; R.& B.I., p. 208;
2. Vide *A.N.* pp. 348-49.
3. *R & B,* p. 127.
4. Waris, Or 1675. Fol. 1426-143 b.
5. *Ain* , J, II, p. 249
6. Vide Saran, *Provincial Government,* pp. 118-120.
7. *Ibid.*, pp. 120-21.

9

The Zamindars in the Sub-Himalayan Ranges

Apart from their domination in the plains, Mughals endeavoured to assert their authority even in the sub-Himalayan ranges from the Northwest to the East. From Akbar's reign onwards, the native hill principalities established since ages and with a long political checkered career were brought under the Mughal pattern of *Zimmidari* system.[1] Some of these principalities own their origin to the pre-Christian times, others to the early centuries of the Christian era, while a few even to the 15th and 16th centuries A.D. Regarding the rajput principalities, Sir Denzil Ibetson remarks, "Rajput dynasties with pedigrees more ancient and unbroken than can be shown by any other royal families in the world."[2]

Authoritative works in the local history of Kashmir and the Punjab Hill states have been produced on the basis of Kalhana's Rajatarangini (tr. Stein), *Vansavalis* (family histories), epigraphical and archaeological sources and along with the Muslim chronicles of medieval India.[3]

Apart from the chronicles, original documents are still available with some of the ruling families in these principalities which bring out the true character of their relationship with the Mughal State.[4]

The history of these independent and semi-independent principalities definitely enters a new phase with the acceptance of the Mughal authority. In essence, their relationship with the Mughal State was based on the same principles as in Rajasthan or elsewhere. By far, the largest of the Hill Chiefs, known hitherto, the *Zimmidars*[5] with varying degrees in territorial extent and material sources submitted to the Mughal authority. On submission, invariably a substantial portion of the property was attached to the Mughal State being put in the *tankhwa jagir* to any Mughal State official and the rest of the territory was assigned in personal *jagir* to the *Zimmidar*. In some cases, a *Zimmidar* was enrolled as *Mansabdar* and apart from his *watan jagir* was assigned the rest of his own territory in the declared *tankhwa jagir* territory of any other *Zimmidari*. Even when not enrolled as *Mansabdar*, the local chief was obliged to render military service like any other provincial *Zimmidar*. Moreover, every *Zimmidar* had to pay a fixed amount of *nazrana* or *peshkash* to the Mughal State. Every *Zimmidar* was subject to confirmation by the Mughal State. On accession, a *Zimmidar* had to pay *nazrana,* after which he received a *Kharita* (a patent of Installation), recognition of *Tikka* along with a *Khilat* (dress of honour and gifts). Any boundary dispute between the *Zimmidaries* was subject to arbitration by the Mughal State.[6] Though always subject to the Mughal *Zimmidari* regulations, it cannot be denied that at times, helped by the isolated and mountaineous rugged character rendering a Mughal invasion, especially during the monsoons and snowy weather, a difficult one, some of the ambitious *Zimmidars* indulged in the private warfare violating the mutual territorial boundaries. But the Mughal machinery was always effectively enforced to keep them under Mughal submission in conformity with the succession rules, *jagir* regulation and the exaction of the *peshkash.* Some of the *Zimmidari* areas were reduced *amli* whereas others remained *ghair amli.* At the time, like the Rajasthan chiefs, the Hill *Zimmidars* also enjoyed administrative and judicial authonomy within their *Zimmidaries* and full revenue powers in assessment and collection in the *ghair amli* territories.

In Shahjahan's reign, the *Faujdar* of the Kangra division realised 4 *lacs* of rupees as *peshkash* from the *Zimmidars.*[7] As a guarantee for loyalty, a *Zimmidar* had to send a member of the family as a hostage at the Imperial Court of Delhi. In the beginning of Jahangir's reign, there were 22 Rajput princes from the Punjab Hills held as hostages at the Mughal Court.[8] In their *watan jagir* areas, the *Zimmidars* were free to make any religious rent-free grant of land.[9]

For the maintenance of the Mughal control over the hereditary chiefs, *Faujdars* were appointed at strategic stations, each *Jagirdar's* territorial jurisdiction comprising a circle of a few *Zimmidaries* and was responsible for the enforcement of the Mughal authority and exacting the *peshkahs* (*nazrana*) from the subdued *Zimmidaries*. The numerous native *Zimmidaries* of the outer ranges of the Punjab Himalayas ranging from the Indus to the sources of the Ganges were divided into the Western, Central and the Eastern groups, with centres located at Kashmir, Jammu and Kangra respectively.[10] Under the Mughals, after the conquest of Kashmir in 1586 A.D., the Western group was attached with the *Sarkar* of

Kashmir (*Subah* Kabul or from Shahjahan's reign onward, a separate *Subah* of Kashmir). The Central and the eastern ranges were attached with the *Subah* of Lahore with *Faujdari* divisions located at Jammu and Kangra respectively.[11] The comparative larger source material for the Kangra Group demanding parity in exemption shall bear out the main traits of the relationship between the Mughal State and the Hill Chiefs.

The Kangra Group comprised the *Zimmidaries* of Kangra, Guler, Jaswan (Jason and Rajpura), Nurpur (Pathankot Dhameri), Chamba, Suket, Mandi, Kulu, Lahul Banghal and Bilaspur. All these chieftainships of the Kangra range were subdued in Akbar's reign and a substantial portion from each of these proportionate to their area was attached to the Mughal State for assignment in *tankhaw jagir* to the Mughal officers.[12] But several expeditions against the Hill Chiefs in Akbar's reign show that the segregation of Kangra proper and some of the other areas was not complete and was later fully accomplished only in Jahangir's reign.[13]

Nagarkot

The Kangra Chief, Raja Dharm Chand (1528 A.D.-1563 A.D.) accepted Akbar's supremacy in the very first year of his reign.[14] His successor, Raja Manikya Chand (1563-1570 A.D.) remained uneventful but his successor Raja Jai Chand (1570-1605 A.D.), having incurred the Emperor's displeasure, was confined to Delhi and the territory of Kangra was assigned in *tankhwa jagir* to Raja Bir Bai.[15] As the minor Raja Bidhi Chand put under the charge of Raja Gobind Chand Jaswal was equally disobedient in 1572 A.D., Khan Jahan Hussain Quli Khan, the Governor of the Panjab, besieged the Kangra Fort and after peace negotiations, forced Raja Gobind Jaswal to personal submission, and Raja Bir Bai was to be adequately compensated for having received his revenues in *tankhwa jagir*. Before the Fort surrendered, K. J. Hussain Quli was obliged to offer terms through negotiations as Mirza Ibrahim Hussain had invaded the Panjab.[16] Again in 1579 A.D., Raja Todar Mal enforced submission and assigned to Mughal forces some areas from the Kangra territory in *tankhwa jagir*.[17] As the Kangra Chiefs often remained recalcitrant, the Fort was finally conquered by Jahangir in 1620 A.D.[18] The major portions of the Kangra territories were annexed to the Mughal State, leaving some portion with the family of Raja Hari Chand in personal *jagir*.[19] The *Zimmidari* of Kangra continued in existence throughout the Mughal age though Raja Hari Chand and his successors, Raja Bhan Chand and Vijai Ram Chand continued to be recalcitrant.[20] But Udai Ram Chand fully accepted Aurangzeb's authority and his *jagir* was increased.[21] His sucessors, too, Bhim Chand, Alam Chand and Hamir Chand continued to be loyal *Zimmidars*.[22]

Gwalior (Guler)

Raja Jagidish Chander accepted Akbar's authority[23] and was enlisted as a loyal *Zimmidar*. One of his successors, Raja Rup Chand, actively served Jahangir in his Kangra campaing and was assigned half of his *Zimmidari* in free gift (*inam jagir*) and the remaining half as *tankhwa jagir* but the *pargana* of Guler was declared *amli*.[24] Later on, his relation with Shahjahan became acrimonious and he was subdued by a Mughal expedition.[25] His successor, Raja Man Singh, served under Aurangzeb in the siege of Qandhar. After that, his successor Raja Bikarm Singh held *mansabs* under Aurangezeb and remained faithful.[26]

Jaswan

The *Zimmidari* of Jaswan, comprising also the *pargana* of Rajpura finds mention in the *Ain* as *amli* areas[27] and remained subject to the Mughal rule from Akbar to Aurangzeb with intermittent violence in the ealier stage.[28]

Darmeri (Nurpur)

The ancient principality of Darmeri (Nurpur)[29] was bounded on the North by Chamba, on the east by Kangra and Guler, on the South by the Panjab plains, and on the west by the Ravi.[30] Abul Fazl designated the Chief as the *Zimmidar* of Mau and Paithan. In 1557 A.D., Akbar reduced the Fort of Kalanaur and overpowered Bhakt Mal who had supported Sikander Sur and replaced him by his brother Takht Mal.[31] Bhakt Mal (1558-80 A.D.) remained faithful to Akbar but his successor Raja Bas Dev, though enrolled as a *Mansabdar*, rebelled numerous times against Akbar.[32] He held a *mansab* of 1500 under Akbar.

The *Zimmidari* comprised the *Parganas* of Mau, Dharmeri, Pathan (Kot) and Shahpur. Apart from some territory assigned in *watan jagir*, the major portions were attached to the Mughal administration for revenues. *Ain* puts the native *Parganas* of Kharmeri and Mau as *Ghair Amli* whereas the *Parganas* of Pathan and Shahpur are Shown *amli*.[33] After the suppression of the revolt in 1594-95, the *Pargana* of Pathankot was given to Mirza Rustam Khan Qandhari.[34] As the members of the ruling family were *Mansabdars* of the Mughal State, they could as well hold their own full territory or a part thereof in *tankhwa jagir*. Raja Suraj Mal (1613-18 A.D.) after recognition by Jahangir, was conferred the rank of 2000 *zats* and *sawars* and the *Pargana* of his own *Zimmidari* in *tankhwa jagir*.[35] His successor Jagat Singh held a commanding position as a Mughal *Mansabdar* under Jahangir and Shah Jahan though his personal career was not free from occasional refractory behavior.[36] In 1627 A.D., on Shah

Jahan's accession, he held the *mansab* of 3000 *zats* and 2000 *sawars* and was confirmed in rank. He served in the Mughal army at various places. In 1637 A.D., he commanded an army against the Persians in Qandhar and in 1638 A.D., was appointed as the *Faujdar* of lower and upper Bangash (Kurrum and Khhat).[37] In 1640 A.D., he was appointed by Shah Jahan as the *Faujdar* of the entire Kangra range responsible for the realization of the 4 *lacs* of Rupees as *peshkash* from all the *Zimmidaris* under the Kangra *Faujadari* division.[38]

As to his own refracting behaviour, he attached himself with Prince Khurrum's rebellion against Jahangir[39] and was pardoned through the intervention of Nur Jahan Begum.[40] He also tried to extend his territories and influence over Chamba, Guler and Suket even in defiance of the Mughal authorities.[41] Having been pardoned in 1645 A.D., he was attached with Ali Mardan Khan against Balkh and Bakshan and died at Kabul in 1646 A.D.[42]

His successors Raja Rajrup Singh, Raja Mandhata and Dayadhata also held *mansabs* and assigned important posts in the reigns of Shah Jahan and Aurangzeb. Raja Rup Singh (1646-61 A.D.), on accession to *Gadi*, was given *mansab* of 1500 *zats* and 1000 *sawars* and also appointed as the *Faujdar* of Kangra division.[43] Later on, after his services in Balkh and Badkshan, his *mansab* was increased to 2000 *zats* and 1500 *sawars*[44] and in 1649 A.D., raised to 2500 *zat* and *sawars*.[45] He provided help to Dara against Aurangzeb but later on kept neutral in the war of succession.[46] Aurangzeb raised his rank to 3500 *zats* and *sawars* and took charge of Chandi in Garhwal against Sulaiman Shikoh[47] to coerce Raja Prithvi Pal, who gave shelter to Sulaiman[48] and in 1661 A.D., was appointed *Thanadar* of Ghazni.[49] His successor, Raja Mandhata (1661-1700) after 20 years' service inside Nurpur, was given the rank of 2000 *zats & sawars*. The last chief under Aurangzeb was Raja Dayadhata (1700-35).

Shahpur

In 1650 A.D., Shah Jahan had detached the *Pargana* of Shahpur from the *Zimmidari* of Nurpur and bestowed it on Bhan Singh, younger son of Jagat singh, as a separate Chiefship with capital at Shahpur.[50] Bhan Singh's descendants remained in this possession throughout the Mughal period. They remained in possession till 1781 when it was dismembered between the Nurpur and the Sikh chiefs.[51]

Chamba

Raja Partap Singh Varman of the ancient principality of Chamba after submission to Akbar's authority, was assigned some portion in personal *jagir* whereas the area of Rihlu and its Eastern territory along with small districts of Chari and Gharoh, lately acquired from Kangra, were surrendered to the Mughal State for revenue administration.[52] *Ain* mentions Chamba as an *amli* territory.[53] The *Zimmidars* of Chamba remained faithful to the Mughal State.[54] In Shah Jahan's reign, Raja Prithvi Singh was enrolled as a regular *Mansabdar* and was awarded extra *jagirs* in *tankhwa.*[55] According to the Chamba Chronicle, he was awarded a *jagir* in Jaswan, of Rs. 16,000 which continued with the family for 90 years. The *jagir* comprised Dun and Nandaun in Kangra.[56] He also, with the help of Sangram Pal of Basholi, fought against and overpowered Jagat Singh of Nurpur who had rebelled against Shah Jahan. His successors Chatar Singh (1664-1690 A.D.) and Udai Singh (1690-1720 A.D.) had some unpleasantness with Aurangzeb. Chatar Singh recovered the *Pargana* of Bhalai from the Chief of Basholi and got a Royal *Sanad* in his favour.[57]

Suket & Mandi

Ain covers Suket and Mandi as one principality though they were two different principalities.[58] Suket and Mandi were always rivals of each other. Evidently, like other *Zimmidaries*, both Suket and Mandi came under Akbar's control though the first regular reference for their allegince occurs in early Shah Jahan's reign.[59] Later, Aurangzeb summoned Raja Shyam Sen of Suket and his brother Naurang Singh to Lahore and ordered them to capture a strong fortress in which they were successful. As a reward, apart from *Khilat* (Dress of honour) etc., the Chief was granted the permission to issue his own coinage. The *Zimmidari* of Mandi lost some of its territories to the Raja of Kulu.[60] Similarly, the *Mandi Annals* show Mandi to have been under the Mughal control in Akbar's reign.[61]

Kulu

Kulu does not find any mention in the *Ain* but the original documents of the reigns of Shah Jahan and Aurangzeb treat Raja Jagat Singh, the *Zimmidar* of Kulu in subordination for the Mughal authority like any other Hill *Zimmidar.*[62] A *Nishan* of Dara Shikoh, dated 1657 A.D., ordered Jagat Singh to restore the disputed territory of Raja Jog Chand.[63]

Another *Farman* of Aurangzeb, dated 1658 A.D. , requires Jagat Singh to join hands with Dhan Chand Khahluria of Bilaspur, to close the roads through the hills against Sulaiman Shikoh, son of Dara Shikoh, who sought to rejoin his father.[64] A similar order was sent to Raja Suhag Parkash of Sirmour and to Raja Rup Singh of Nurpur.[65]

The territory of Lahul was subject to the principality of Kulu[66] which also exacted tribute from Spiti.[67]

Bilaspur

Ain does not mention Bilaspur. All the same, the local *Annals* put the chieftainship under the Mughal subordination since Raja Gyan Chand's (1570-1600 A.D.) submission to Akbar.[68] Gyan Chand also mentions Raja Dip Chand to have been in Aurangzeb's service as *Mansabdar.* Dip Chand was despatched by Aurangzeb in an expedition to Northwest Frontier and received a present of 5 *lacs* of Rupees.[69]

Kutlehr

Similarly, Kutlehr is not mentioned in *Ain* or any other Mughal chronicle but the original Mughal *Sanads* granted to the *Rais* of Kutlehr clearly put them under the *Zimmidari* category, on the payment of *peshkash* and rendering of the military service.[70] The territory of Kutlehr Chauki, Kutlehr Mankhandi in Nadaun and Talhati, now in Hoshiarpur, is at present a *taluqa* in Kangra division.

Jammu Circle

The central circle of the Punjab Himalayan range comprised the principalities of Jammu, Mankot, Jasrota, Bhadrawah, Lakhanpur, Chaneri, Basohli, Bhadu and Kashtwar. All these submitted to the Mughal authority in Akbar's reign and were brought within the *Zimmidari* regulations. The *Faujdari* of the Jammu division had jurisdiction over all these hill *Zimmidaris* besides maintaining Mughal control over them, and realized *peshkash* and enforced *jagir* regulations.[71] Of these, *Ain* mention Jammu, Mankot, Jasrota and Bhadu as fulfledged *amli Parganas* and Bahadarwah as *ghair amli.*[72] The *Zimmidars* of these territories also find mention in *Ain* in connection with their revolts in the 35th year (1588-89 A.D.) by Zain Khan and ultimate reduction for submission and payment of revenues.[73]

After the final subjection of the Hill Chieftainships by Akbar, they seemed to have settled down into comparative quiet submission. Sangram Dev of Jammu served Jahangir faithfully[74] and sent the forces for the suppression of revolt in Kashtwar.[75]

Unlike the Eastern group, for want of original records, it is difficult to state as to how much area was left with each *Zimmidar* in personal *jagir* and the area passed on to Mughal territory for the realisation of direct revenues. All the same, some stray references state about the fate of some of the *Zimmidaries*. The fate of the *Parganas* of Samba and Josotra was referred to the Emperor for disposal[76] whereas Lakhanpur was passed in *jagir* to Muhammad Khan Turkoman.[77] Bhoti was a dependency of Jammu.[78]

The Mughal rule was fully respected for the reshuffling in the *jagir* assignment in these *Zimmidari* areas. Jahangir transferred the areas of Shahpur-Kandi from Nurpur to Basohli[79] and later constituted them into a separate *Zimmidari.*

In early Aurangzeb's reign, the Mughal State enforced the transfer of disputed *Pargana* of Bhalia from Basohli to Chamba and assigned the revenues of the *Zimmidaries* of Bhadrawah to Chamba.[80] Prithvi Singh of Chamba had made an appeal to the Imperial Court in 1648 A.D. and an enquiry was made by the *Subhahdar* of Lahore. The decision was confirmed by a *Sanad* issued by Mir Khan, *Subahadar* of Lahore, dated 18th March, 1661 A.D.[81]

Kashmir itself was conquered by Akbar in 1586 A.D. and constituted into a *Sarkar* of *Subah* Kabul.[82] The *Zimmidaries* of the Western side of the Central Punjab Himalayan group, Kahtwar, Rajauri, Punch, Kotla, Bhimbhaar, Khari Khariyal were all Mohemmadan *Zimmidaries* with the exception of Kashtwar. Though they had been historically associated with Kashmir, they were attached to the *Subah* Punjab for administration.[83]

The *Zimmidari* of Kashtwar was finally subdued by Jahangir and Gunwar Singh was entrusted with the *jagir* of Kashtwar with the title of *Raja* on the condition of allegiance, payment of *peshkash* (revenues) and sending his son as a hostage to the Mughal Court.[84] In 1619 A.D., Dilawar Khan, the Governor of Kashmir, conqured Kashtwar. Jahangir made favourable comments on the reliability of Raja Gunwar Singh, ordered his release from the Gwalior Fort and reinstated him as the *Zimmidar* with gifts and the title of *Raja.* Thereafter, the Kashtwar *Zimmidars* remained faithful to the Mughal State and observed the *Zimmidari* regulations.[85] In 1629 A.D. in Shahjahan's reign, Bhagwan Singh, younger son of Gunwar Singh, served Shahjahan in Deccan.[86] Kirat Singh (1681-1728 A.D.) embraced Islam with the name of Saadat Yar Khan.[87]

The Raja of Rajauri, Sir Mast Khan, sunmitted to Mughal authority when the Mughal forces, while passing through Rajauri, marched against Kashmir and also rendered military help against Kashmir in lieu of which he was confirmed in his *Zimmidari* along with *jagir* in Kashmir.[88] Jahangir passed through Rajauri numerous times, and ordered the *Zimmidar* to build '*Chaukis*' (watch posts) and post guards all along the route to Kashmir in his *Zimmidari*[89] (Jahangir also gives part of his own comments on the people of Rajauri) and also called upon the *Raja* to furnish a contingent for an expedition against Baltistan placed under the command of his son, Inayat Ullah Khan.[90] Inayat Ullah Khan, the *Raja* of Rajauri, participated in the War of Succession as an ally of Aurangzeb and in lieu of the services was confirmed in Kashmir again and was awarded the fresh *jagirs* of Punch,

Samlah, Manawar, Khari Kharyali and Bhimbar.[91] In the *Ain,* Bhimbar and Kharyali are stated as *amli parganas.*[92]

The *Zimmidars* were granted personal *jagirs* whereas the rest of their territories were assigned in *tankhwa jagir* to the Mughal officials or to the other *Zimmidars.*[93] *Ain* mentions the grant of Siyurgal in the *Pargana* of Khariyali which shows that the revenues of the territory other than the personal *jagirs* of the *zimmidars* were attached to the Mughal administration for further assignments. Later on, Aurangzeb conferred the revenues of these territories to the Raja of Rajauri.[94]

Footnotes

1. It is not within the scope of the present work to describe the past political history of the principalities.

2. Ibbeston, D., *Punjab Castes*, Lahore, 1916, p. 54.

3. For the local details of political history, pre-Mughal History and Pre-Mughal Age, see Tod, '*Annals*', Cunningham Alexander's "*Ancient Geography of India, Reports of the Archaeological Survey of India,*" Vol. I-XXIII; Dutt, R.C., "*A History of Civilisation of Ancient India.*" 2 vols.'; Drew, F. "*The Jammu &Kashmir Territories,*"; Dutt, J.C., "*Kings of Kashmir*"; Mohibul Hasan, "*Kashmir under the Sultanate*"; Fleet, J.D.,"*Corpus Inscriptionum Indicarum,*" Vol. xiii; Francke, A.H., "*A History of Western Tibet, Antiquities of Indian Tibet*"; Griffin, Lepel H., "*The Punjab Chiefs, The Rajas of the Punjab*" Haarcourt, A.F.D., "*The Himalayan District*"; Ibbeston, D.C, "*Outlines of Punjab Ethnography*"; Latif, S.M., "*History of the Punjab*"; J. Hutchinson & J. Ph. Vogel, "*The History of the Punjab Hill States*". "*District Gazetteers* and *Settlement Reports*".

4. For this purpose, unlike the Rajasthan Archives, which I scrutinized myself, I have relied on the Mughal *Farmans* and some quoted by the *Settlement Reports and District Gazetteers* based on personal study on the part of the respective authors who had an access to the family Archives of various *Rajas*. Though the authors have invariably quoted them in the context of the political history, I have drawn upon them for administrative analyses with references in the footnotes.

5. Sir J.B. Lyall, *Kangra Settlement Report,* p. 191. "The Mughal emperors, in communication asddressed to the Hill Rajas, gave them the title of *Zimmindars* i.e. land holders. Documents are preserved in the Rajas' families in which this address is used."

6. *Chamba Gazetteer,* p. 85 refers to a *Sanad* of the reign of Shah Jahan, regarding a boundary dispute between Prithvi Singh of Chamba (AD 1641-64) and Sangram-Pal of Balor, about the *Pargana* of Bhalai, which was claimed by both states. The dispute was settled by a second *sanad* in the reign of Aurangzeb in favour of Chamba, and by an Imperial Officer to whom the duty had been entrusted by the Emperor.

7. Refer to Jat Singh appointment vide Amil Sahib II, p. 3330. 13th regnal year; Abdul Hamid Lahori, *Padshahnama,* pp. 237-38.

8. See *Tuzuk-i-Jahangiri*; Cunningham, *Chamba Gazetteer*, p. 88. The word '*Mian*' meaning Prince was coined by Jahangir for the Rajput Hill Princes held as hostages.

9. For the period of Balabhadra, the Raja of Chamba (1589-1621 A.D.) Cunningham discovered 42 copper plates bestowing grants of land and gifts on *Brahmans* and temples. Such grants have also been discovered in Nurpur and Kangra for the Mughul period. Vide Hutchinson pp. 299-301. A copper plate of Balbhadra dated 1618 A.D. confers a religious grant on the *Parohit* of Raja Jagat Singh of Nurpur.

10. According to Sir Alexander Cunningham vide *Ancient Geography of India*, Vol. I, p. 130, et seq. The three-fold pre-Mughal classical of the Principalities into Western Group of Kashmir, Central Group of Dugar (Jammu) and the Eastern Group of Trigarta (Kangra) was an old one. These groups had formed confederation on feudal lines since ancient times. For details, see Cunningham, *Ibid.*).

11. *Jahangir Memoirs*, tr. Vol. I, pp. 49 and 65.

12. *Akbarnama* (*AN*) II, p. 358. Tr. Beveridge mentions that in the 23rd year (1579 A.D.) Raja Todar Mal arranged the *jagirs* of the officers of the Kachwaha family in the Punjab and resuppressed some of the refracting Chiefs in the Hills. "He (Todar Mal) was also ordered....Hill Proprietors (*Zimmidars*)...punished and banished." (vide *Kangra Settlement Report*, 1889, p. 8). Mr. Barnes comments that Todar Mal having accomplished the task reported to the Emperor that he had to cut off the meat and left the line", i.e. he had attached the fertile tracts and left only the bare hills to the Hill Chiefs.

13. Refer tot he revolt in 1620 AD. Revolt in the part of the Hill Chiefs on a large Scale—conquest of Kangra—*Tuzki Jahangiri*.

14. When Akbar's forces pursued Sikander Sur into the Siwalik Hills, Raja Dharm Chand and variours other *Zimmidars* paid homage. T.A. Elliott, p. 248 erroneously gave the name of Raja Ram Chand who was in fact the father of Dharm Chand.

15. *A.N.* III, p. 6, Cawnpur, edition, *M.U.I*, pp. 647-48.

16. For the political details and terms, see *A.N.* Cawnpur, ed. Vol. II, p. 6; T.A. Elliott, V, p. 356; *M.U.* Blochmann, Vol. I, pp. 647-48.

17. *A.N.* II, p. 358, tr. Bev., *Kangra Settlement, 1889*, p. 8 notes that the portion of the areas taken from the Kangra seems to have been sixty-six villages in valley.

18. Raja Triloka Chand (1605-12 A.D.) and Raja Hari Chand (1612-1627 A.D.) and Raja Chander Bhan Chand (1627-1660 A.D.) were contemporaries of Jahangir. For details of the relations with the Rajas and the conquest of Kangra, see *Tuzk-i-Jahangiri,* Vol. I (tr. Rogers and Beveridge), pp. 283, 301, 311, 324, 326, 336, 361-62, 388, 392-93; *Shah Fateh-i-Kangra,* Elliott, vol. VI, pp. 521-26; *M.U.* II, pp. 166-168, 184-8-185, 238.

19. *Kangra Settlement Report, 1889,* p. 8, notes that only the *Pargana* of Rajgir (on the right bank of Bias, above Alampur including Lambagraon, Jaisinghpur and Bijapur) was assigned to the ruling family in personal *jagir*. The rest of the territory was put under Mughal administration. In 1889 A.D., Mr. Barnes (*Ibid.*, p.8) found *sanads* still extant, issued between the reigns of Akbar and Aurangzeb, appointing individuals to various judicial and revenue offices.

20. *Tarikh-i-Punjab* vide *Kangra Annals,* p. 72. Raja Bhan Chand was captured and flayed in Jahangir's reign. Mian Bhan Chand (1627 A.D.-1660 A.D.)

was captured in Aurangzeb's reign; Vijai Ram Chand ruled from 1660 A.D.-1687 A.D.)

21. *Tarikh-i-Punjab* based on *Kangra Annals*. Apart from the *jagir* of Rajgir, five other *taluqas* viz. Nadaun, Palam, Mahal-Sarai, Jaisukh and Mahar were added.

22. Udhai Ram Chand (1687 A.D.-1690 A.D.; Bhim Chand, 1690-1697; Alam Chand (1697-1700 A.D; Hamir Chand, 1700-1747 A.D.; also refer to *Kangra Settlement Report* and Cunningham.

23. T.A. Elliott, V, p. 357.

24. (a) Vide *Ain* II, p. 322; *Tuzk.* Tr. Vol. 1. (b) Jagdish Chander (1570-1605 A.D.); Vijay Chand (1605-1610 A.D.) Rup Chand (1610-1661 A.D.). *Tuzk.* Tr. Vol. II, pp.. 187,191,289; (c) As Jahangir comments, "As Raja Rup Chand of Gwalior had been very active in his service at Kangra, an order was given to the Chief Diwans to hand over half of his native place to him in free gift, and the remaining half as a *tankhwa jagir*."

25. Refer to expedition of Srinagar in 1634 A.D.; capital of Guler—vide Amil Salib; *Tarikh Shah Jahani,* 13th Regnal Year, p. 108.

26. Raja Bikram Singh (1661-1675 A.D.) held *mansab* of 2500 *zat* and *sawars* and was appointed *Thanadar* of the Kangra Hills. Raja Singh (1675-1695 A.D.); Dalip Singh (1695-1730 A.D.).

27. Vide *Ain*, II, p. 320.

28. Raja Gobind Chand of Jaswan was an ally of Raja Bidhi Chand, minor son of Raja Jai Chand of Kangra at the siege of Kangra by Hussain Quli Khan and in negotiations of price settlement with the latter in 1572 A.D. The chiefs of Jaswal in Anirudh Chand is mentioned in the revolts of 35th year (1588-89); vide *Ain.* I, p. 344; *M.U.* II, p. 60; *A.N.* Elliott, Vol. IV, pp. 126-129.

29. The old Hindu name of Nurpur was Darmeri or Dharmeri, which is not an impossible abbreviation of Andumbara. The name was changed to Nurpur by Jahangir in honour of wife, Nur Jahan. Vide. *Punjab Survey Report,* Vol. XIV, 1878-79, pp. 115-119.

30. Kangra G., p. 28. It originally included Pathankot and a large tract on the plain—now in Jammu State. Hutchinson, I, p. 213.

31. Bhakt Mal (1513-58 A.D.) gave shelter to Sikander Sur and assisted him in the defence of the Fort of Kalanour but his defeat was put to death by Bharam Khan in 1558 A.D. vide *M.U.* II, 157.

32. He rebelled in 1585 A.D. vide *Tuzk*, tr. II, p. 266; *B.N* II, p. 287; in 35th year (1589-90 A.D).; *Ain,* I, p. 344; and in 41st year (1594-95 A.D.) and in 1603-04 A.D. vide *M.U.* II, pp. 167-170; *Ibid.*, p. 160.

33. *Ain,* II, p. 322. All these *Parganas* are a part of Sarkar Bari Doab, *Subah* Lahore.

34. *M.U.* II, p. 367. (chk. *Akbar Nama*).

35. *Waqiat-i-Jahangiri* vide Elliott, VI, p. 374; *M.U.* II, 176-177.
36. *M.U.* II, p. 239.
37. Vide *B.N.* II, p. 237.
38. *B.N.* II, p. 238.
39. Vide *Tuzk-Jahangir*, II, p. 226.
40. *Ibid.*, p. 289.
41. *B.N.* II, pp. 237-318; *Chamba Gazetteer*, pp. 88-89, 90-93.
42. Vide *B.N.* II, pp. 451, 463, 481.
43. *M.U.* II, p. 277.
44. *Ibid.*, 277-f.
45. *Ibid.*
46. Mannucci, tr. Irvine, I, p. 310.
47. *M.U.* II, p. 278.
48. *Alamgirnamah*, p. 190-199.
49. *Ibid.*
50. Shahpur comprised the territory from the west of Chaki River to River Ravi.
51. Gurdas G., p. 18.
52. Ref. Cunningham and *Chamba Gazetteer*.
53. *Ain*, II. J, p. 324 in Sarkar Rechna Duab. (Cultivalbe area: 6,021 *Bighas* 6 *Biswas*, Revenues 4, 548,000 *dam*, Infantry 100, Cavalry 1000.)
54. Jahangir, while describing his campaign against Kangra comments, "At this stage the offering of the Raja of Chamba... patronage and favour." (Hutchinson, pp. 300-303, named in the original *State Annals*); Here, Jahangir definitely indulges in self praise and exaggeration. There is no denying that in the Kangra Hills, the situation was sufficiently favoureble for him all the same, Chamba had already submitted in Akbar's reign. Raja Baalabhadra (1589-1611 A.D.) and Raja Janardan (1618-21 A.D.) remained faithful to the Mughal State and even fought wars against Raja Jagat Singh of Nurpur. On Janardan's death in 1621, the principality remained subject to Jagat Singh of Nurpur. (vide Hutchinson, p. 302) Prithvi Raj (1641-64 A.D.) was enrolled in 1641 A.D. as the *Mansabdar* of 1000 *Z & S* under Shah Jahan. (Vide *Badshahnama*, p. 81)
55. B.N. Prithvi Chand in 1641 A.D.—1664 A.D.
56. Also see *Kangra Settlement Report.*
57. Bhuri Singh Museum catalogue Appendix IV, C. 1,2,3,4.
58. *Ain.* J. p. 321- with cultivable land 42,152 *Bighas*, 1680,000 *Dam.*, revenues, 200 *Sawars* and 8000 *cavalry* under Somliansi Rajputs. Also, *Kangra Settlement Report*, p. 8; L. Griffin, '*The Rajas of the Panjab*', p. 579.

59. Vide *Suket Annals*. Hutchinson, pp. 353-54.

60. Hutchinson, pp. 355-56 based on *Annals*.

61. *Kangra Settlement Report*, p. 8; Hutchinson, II, p. 380. The *Annals* also state that the Peshkash was fixed through Raja Jagat Singh, *Faujdar* of Kangra in 1640-41 A.D.; Hutchinson, II, p. 382.

62. *Archeological Survey,* 1907-08, p. 268-270; quote 13 *Farmans* between 1650-58.

63. *Archeological Survey Report* 1907-08 p. 268 quotes the *Nishan* "if from obstinance and imprudence... annihilate him"; Huthinson, p. 460.

64. *Archeological Survey, Ibid.*, p. 268; Also Bernier, Vol. 1, p. 84; Also Manucci, I, p. 271.

65. Ch. *Sirmur Gazetteer,* p.13.

66. Vide Jesuit Father A zerdo in 1631 A.D. who passed through Lahul on his way from Leh to the Panjab Plains, Hutchinson, p. 479.

67. Hutchinson, pp 486.

68. Hutchinson, II, p. 499.

69. Hutchinson, p. 502.

70. Hutchinson, p. 489.

71. *Tarikh-i-Shah Jahani*, Mohd. Sadiq, 7th reg. yr, p. 108, mentions Khayanat Khan as the *Faujdar* of Jammu Division over the *Zamindars* of the Punjab Sub-Hills.

72. *Ain*, J. (?) II, pp. 323-324—Jammu, cultivated area: 19,329 *Bighas*; 11 *Biswa*, *Revenue* 3,956,000 *dams*, 1000 *cavalry*, 20,000 *infantry*; Jasorota 15, 430 *Bighas*, 1,150,000 *dams*, 400 *cavalry*, 500 *infantry*; Mankot included 4 towns, 1,312 *Bighas*, 85,119 *dams*, 30 *cavalry*, 1200 *infantry*; Bhadvan—*Bighas* not mentioned—revenue 240,000; 50 *cavalry*, 4000 *infantry*. Bhadhu—See *Ain*. P. 325.

73. *A.N. M.U.* II, pp. 367-68 mentions revolt on the part of the *Zimmidars* of these territories and their suppression by Zain Khan Koka in 1588-89 A.D. and another revolt in 1594-95 suppression by Shaikh Farid (vide *A.N.* Elliott, VI, pp. 125-129).

74. *Tuzk-i-Jahangiri*, vol. II, p. 5, 88, 120,138,154,171,175,193).

75. *Waqia-i-Jahangiri,* Elliot, pp. 373-74.

76. *A.N.* Elliot, VI, pp. 126,27,28

77. *Ibid.*, p. 128.

78. Hutchinson, pp. 576-577.

79. Vide *Annals*; Hutchinson, p. 599

80. *Ibid.*, p. 66, C.#.

81. Vide *Catalogue Chamba Museum*, pp. 52,66. Nos. C1-2, *Chamba Gazetteer*, pp. 92-94.

82. *Ain.,* See details, Mohibul Hassan, *Kashmir under the Sultan.*

83. Cunningham associates him with Jammu Circle for administration.

84. *Tuzk-i-Jahangir*, Vol. II, pp. 135-140, 170.

85. *Ibid.*, Jahangir recognised Jagat Singh as the *Tikka* to Gunwar Singh.

86. Vide *Local Annals.* Hutchinson, p. 651.

87. Vide *Local Annals.* Drew, Jammu & Kashmir, p. 119.

88. Local Annals—*Jagir* is of Rs. 50,000 in Kashmir. The *Raja* made obedience to Akbar in person while on the former's visit to Kashmir in 1586 A.D. vide *Local Annals*. Hutchinson, p. 685—At that time, the principality comprised territory with Pir Panjabi in the North, Bhimliar in South, Chinab in the East and Punch to the West) and was under Samrat Khan (1580-1600 A.D.).

89. *Tuzk,* Vol. II, pp. 180-81.

90. *Ibid.*, p. 189.

91. *Sanads*, quoted in *Chronicles of Rajauri, Local Annals*, vide Hutchinson, p. 687.

92. *Ain.* J. II., p. 325 mentioned in Sarkar Chenhat Devali—Bhimban—cultivated area; 28,668 *Bighas*, 1,200,000 *dams*; Khariyali 57818 *Bighas*, Revenues 2,643,270 *dams*; Suryurghal, 6,633 *Bighas*, 100 *cavalry*, 2000 *Sawars*.

93. *Ain, Ibid.*, mentions Suryurghal in the *Pargana* of Kharyali.

94. *Jahangir's Memoirs,* tr. i, pp. 49 and 65. It was in 1665 when Rajauri came under proper Mughal occupation.

Jagir System

1

Jagir System

All the arable and cultivated lands were divided into two main categories, the *Khalsa* and *Jagir*. The *Khalsa* lands were administered directly by the State which dealt with the *Riaya* of various types in the villages for the purposes of assessment and collection of land revenue. The *Jagir* lands were assigned to various categories of assignees on different terms. Assignments of various kinds, conditional on service (*Jagir Ba-Mashrut*) and not conditional (*Jagir Bila Mashrut*) in *Inam* (reward) and *Madad-i-Maash* (maintenance grants) for philanthropic and charitable purposes, were made throughout the Mughal age. In all the assigned lands, the assessment work was done by the *Pargana* and varied officials in accordance with the State regulations. All land revenue documents pertaining to the record of rights for the villages (*Muzas*) and the *Pargana* as a whole were prepared by the officials as for the *Khalsa* lands. But the assignees had to employ their own officials and soliders for the collection of land revenue in collaboration with the village and *Tappah* officials, *Muqqadam, Patwari, Chaudhari* and the *Qanungo*.

The *Iqta* or *Jagir* system, both for the remunerations of the service personnel and religious maintenance grants, were known to the Sultanate period and Pre-Akbar Mughal age in India. The principle of responsibility of the State for the entire collection of the land revenue only through direct Governemnt salaried officers is rather a recent phenonema and is a product of the British system of land administration in India. The medieval State, both in the Sultanate and Mughal periods, delegated powers to various intermediaries viz. *Zamindars, Jagirdars* and Revenue Farmers for the collection of the land revenue through the village functionaries. The *Jagir* system was equally known to the Timur's adminstrationjh in Central Asia and other Islamic countries[1]. On his conquest of India, Babar made assignments through his followers at different places and even allowed the obedient *Zamindars* (*Rais* and *Rajas*) with allowance and maintenance[2]. Hamayun confirmed the assignments made by his father and followed tradition[3]. In this respect, Shershah also carried on the same pattern and made frequent grants for service personnel and religious purposes[4]. Having thus inherited, Akbar made the institution of *Jagir* system as a regular feature of his administration, though undeniably his reign and that of his successors witnessed radical modifications for its operation in the Mughal administrative and agrarian polity.

Though Moreland's analysis of the nature of assignments made under Akbar and in the 17th century is quite reliable[5], all the same in matters of details of its working and for want of authentic contemporary evidence, Moreland left various questions either open or inconclusive[6]. The recently discovered documents of the reigns of Shahjahan and Aurangzeb throw flood of light on the various problems connected with the institution of *Jagirdari* in the 17th century. Many of these problems facing the *Jagirdari* were the same as in the earlier two reigns of Akbar and Jahangir and, as such, enable us to equally understand more clearly their nature, known hitherto simply from the general statements in the *Chronicles* or the *Ain*. In this light, some of the views of Moreland based simply either on the chronicles or the accounts of the foreign travellers had to be modified. Besides this, many of the newly discovered religious grants from the reign of Akbar onwards afford a comprehensive view of the nature of the working of the *Madad-i-Maash* administration.

The *Khalsa* and *Saraf-i-Khas* Lands

The Mughal State reserved the revenue of the *Khalsa* lands for the State exchequer. Further, five technical distinctions existed between the *Khalsa* and *Saraf-i-Khas* (or *Khasa Sharifa* lands). The revenue from the latter were reserved for the *Previ*/purse of the rulling monarch. Like the *Khalsa* lands, it had exactly a similar pattern of administration though with distinctly separate staff and treasury.[7] Due to lack of any direct evidence, it is difficult to work out exact ratio between the *Khalsa* and *Saraf-i-Khas* land.

Broadly speaking, the Jagir grant was of two types, *Mashrut* (conditional on service) and *Bila Mashrut* (unconditional) given either as *Inam* (reward) or in *Madad-i-Maash* (maintenance grants).

Tankhaw Jagir

Tankhaw Jagir was always a conditional (*Mashrut*) *Jagir*, contingent on the service rendered to the State. Its State servant could be paid his emoluments in cash (*Naqdi*) or through an assignment named *Tankhaw Jagir*. Whether he was to be paid in cash or in assignment, depended on the pure distinction of monarch. An assignee could as well be paid partly in cash or partly in assignment. Every official was paid salary defined in cash *Dams* and, if put on *Tankhaw Jagir*, was entitled to an assignment of the revenues of an area estimated to yield the income due to him. Invariably, the Mughal State servants-both civil and military-were enrolled as *Mansabdar*. The *Mansabdar* holding a *Jagir*, was assigned revenues both for his personal salary and the salary of the military contignet maintained by him so as to cover *Zat* and *Sawar* ranks. Apart from the assignment of *Jagir* in accordance with the *Mansabdar* scale, a high official may also be granted additional *Jagir* on the condition of sparing 1/3rd of its revenues for the maintenance of the Army for the royal service[8]. However, the paid officials not holding any *Mansab* could also be given *Jagir* assignment in lieu of their salaries. In case the revenues of the assignment either fell short or exceeded the salary claim of an assignee, adjustment was to be done accordingly. In the former case, he was paid the balance in cash and in case the *Jagir* return yielded more, he was required to return the estimated amount to the State named as *Baz Yazft*. At times, he may not be required to return the excessive amount in lieu of which he may be given either proportionate enhancement in *Mansab* and *Jagir* or assigned the same amount in *Inam*.

The assignment was made by the State based on proper survey of the assessment documents. The assignment was made only for the net *Jama* or *Hal-i-hasil* of the villages or the *Mahals*. This denoted the actual returns after having met the incidental collection charges of the local officials and the revenue claims of the *Madad-i-maash* assignees within that area, if any. As already examined, Moreland's interpretation of the *Jama* as valuation and consequently the *Jagirdar's* entire claim on the total *Jamademi* (gross income) is rather inaccurate. Akbar's experiments had gone a long way to bridge the gulf between the *Jama* and the *Hasil* aimed at the fixation of the State demand and consequent valuation. Though in this respect, the *'Jama-Dehsala'* considerably removed the long standing grievance of the assignees, but problem, however, continued to persist more especially in the Deccan throughout the 17th century. Under Shahjahan and Aurangzeb, the regulation of the *Mansabdar* system and the prevalence of the month's scale salaries in proportion to the expected revenue of the *Jagir* assigned clearly point towards the solution of the problem.[9]

The assignment was done by the Revenue Ministry on the basis of the revenue records assessment of valuation prepared by the local revenue officials. The documents of the reign of Shahjahan and Auranzeb clearly show that any variations in the phased valuation and the *Hasil* assigned territories was adjustable. If at the time of assignment, it was ascertained that the *Jama* of the assigned *Mahals* was inflated as against the assigned *Dams*, reduction (names *Takhfif Dami*) was effected in the phased valuation of the *Jagir*[10]. Even after the assignment had been made and accepted, the assignee could claim *Sanad* for reduction if the *Hasil* did not tantamount to the original amount sanctioned for the Jagir. In such a case, the assignee was compenstated for the balance through the grant of either additional *Tankhaw Jagir* for that amount.[11] At times, the adjustment was done by cash payment from the treasury.[12] Similarly, the reduction was afforded in the valuation on account of any sudden fall in the prices or in distribution caused by lawlessness or the remission was effected due to any natural calamity.[13] If the position of the *Hasil* redeemed, the reductions effected could be withdrawn.[14] At the same time, if the actual collection exceeded the sanctioned *Jama* or the monthly ratio sanctioned, the balance named *Baz Yaft* was recoverable from the assignee.[15] At times, the excess amount was not recovered and the assignee, if deserved, was given additional *Sawar* rank and the balance was adjusted in his favour.[16] In order to avoid recurrence of the variations in the valuation and *Hasil* of the assignments, collections were made by periodical inspection of the revenue documents and the changes were made in the month scale ratio.[17]

The salary of a State official, whether *Naqdi* (on cash payment) or a *Jagirdar*, was declared in cash currency of *Dams*, (Forty *Dams* made one Rupee). Notwithstanding the variation in the local currency of some of the provinces in North India, the revenues of *Mahals* in all the Provinces were estimated and declared in *Dams* and Rupees and the assignments were made accordingly. Despite variations in the value of the copper in the 17th century, the *Dam* vs. Rupee ratio of Akbar's reign was maintained right till the end of Aurangzeb's reign for the purposes of land revenue accounts and assignments. A *Mansabdar* holding *Jagir* could be shifted as *Naqdi* (on cash payment)or vice-versa. He could also be paid partly in cash and the rest in *Jagir*. Ordinarily, a *Mansabdar* preferred a good *Jagir* to cash payment. But the preference on the part of some of the *Mansabdars* to be put on cash payment is evident in the last years of Auranzeb's reign when the revenues of some of the assignments dwindled owing to multiple political factors explained later. At times, the State itself put an official as a *Naqdi* if equivalent *Jagir* to the *Tankhwah* of an assignee was not available for the time being. However, ordinarily a *Mansabdar* preferred an assignment of *Jagir* which gave him a traditional sense of self-importance and dignity. Under the treasury rules, on all payments made in cash, a scheduled deduction was made on the sanctioned total amout. But at times, the *Jagirdar* may be exempted from the deduction charges only as a matter of special favour. On *Naqdi*,

Mansabdar was subject to all the rules and regulations of the pardade and review of the contingents maintained by him before getting full salary while as a *Jagirdar*, the flow of his income was uninterrupted. Moreover, if the *Hasil* of a *Jagir* exceeded than the amount sanctioned for his salary on account of any meritorious service, he could expect the balance either in *Inam* or *Tankhwah Jagir* with reciprocal increase in his *Mansab*.

Footnotes

1. *Malfuzat-Timuri* Ms or fol 287, Berlin, *Tiyul-u-Mra* fol 66b; *Inam*, fol 67a, *Surghal, Wazifa* and *Madad-i-Maash* and *Waqf*, fol 76a.
2. *Tuzuk-i-Babri*, tr Bev., pp. 520, 676.
3. *Nafiasul Muassir*, Ms. Rampur, 185b; Ms. Munick, Code Pers. 3, fol 306a.
4. *Abbas*, Ms. Aligh, p. 263; Ms I.O. Fol, 113a.
5. Moreland, *Agrarian System*, pp. 92-100.
6. Dr. P.Saran, in *Provincial Government*, pp. 79-82 has simply relied on Moreland and has added nothing afresh.
7. *Miratul Istilab*, Ms. O.R. 1813, B.M. London, fol. 26a; Ms. K.B. Patna, fol 14b, T.A.Q., Rampur, p. 208, For *Khasa Sharifa*, see *Baharistan*, Suppl. Pers. 252, B.N. Paris, fols 208a, 110b, 160b, 314b, 325b; '*Selected Documents*' p. 60 *Murraqat-i-Hasan*, Rampur, pp. 77, 82, 165, 294; For *Saraf-i-Khas*, see *Raqiam*, Ms. Rampur 132, p. 96/6.
8. R.A.J. *Vakil Report* reg. No. 1303/987 dated 2nd of *Ramzan* 1118 A.H/27th Nov. 1706 A.D., states that the Vakil had submitted an application to the Royal Court regarding the grant of the *Paragana* of Chatsu, Dasua and Mauzabad on the condition that 1/3rd of the revenues of *Parganas* shall be spent on maintaining an Army for the Royal service. Also R.A.J. categories 4, Reg. 970 dated R.Y., 51/1118 A.H.
9. Though the records show this only for the Shahjahan and Aurangzeb, it is not certain if they existed even earlier.
10. S.D.S.R., p. 177; R.A.J. *Akhbarat* No. 1298 dated 27th Rabi I, 10th R.Y. (Aurangzeb) states that the valuations of *Paragna* Faiza Abad alias Makhllaspur was 4 lacs dams. After reduction of 4 lacs, the *Pargana* was assigned to Begum Zaibul Nissa; also *Akhabarat* Reg. No. 1288, dated 10th Rabi I, 10th R.Y. (Aurangzeb.).
11. S.D.S.R., p. 177; R.A.J. Category No. 4 Reg. 164 dated 17th Ramzan, A.H. 1106/1690 A.D. quotes a letter from Megh Raj Vakil to the Maharaja of Amber that Takhfif of 5,000,000 *dams* was granted in the *Parganas* of Maharana Toda and Hindun for a period of two years.
12. *Adabi-i-Alamgiri*, f.155b
13. R.A.J. *Akhbarat*, no. 1288, 10th Rabi I, 10th R.Y. (Aurangzeb) states that Abid Khan was assigned the *Paraganas* of Narnaul and Shahbad (*Subah* Delhi) which were formerly in the *Jagir* of Mohmmed Amin Khan on a 10th month scale *Mansab* when the pricess were high, but later on, the *Parganas* were desolated due to the fall in prices. New assignee i.e., Abid Khan, refused to accept the *Jagir* whereupon the Emperor sanctioned the reduction of 20 lacs *Dams* in valuation; *Akhbarat* no. 1857/ dated 21st Rabi II, 24th R.Y. (*Ibid*), states Ikhlas, Khas, *Faujdar* of Damunai was given *Takhfif* of 8 lacs *Dams* as his sons were looted in the assigned *Jagir* and less realisation in *Hasil* was made on account of the desolation of the territory.

14. R.A.J. category 4, Reg. 1389 dated A.H. 1105/1693 A.D.

15. *Adab* F. 153B

16. R.A.J. *Akhbarat* 12th R.Y.

17. *Akhbarat* 40th R.Y.

2

Administration of Jagir

In his *Jagir*, a Jagirdar exercised revenue powers for the collection of the revenues assigned to him. He had, of course, police and executive powers for the maintenance of the law and orders in his jurisdiction. He had to crush[1] any lawlessness or recalcitrance in his *Jagir* and without such powers for the administration of his *Jagir*, he could not possible realize land revenue from the *ryots*. As such, he could take coercive measures to stamp out any sedition and recalcitrant elements for the non-payment of land revenue.[2] He possessed vast powers for burning and devastating the cultivated fields of the recalcitrants and could seek help from the *Faujdars* and *Karoris* of the assigned areas.[3] He had to arrange for the safety of the roads and the caravans passing through his jurisdiction. In any case or robbery, he had to make good his loss of the caravans.[4] He could also seek help from the *Faujdars* of the divisions and the *Thanedars* of his area.[5]

For the land revenue administration, his powers were strictly confined to the collections of the revenues on the basis of the survey and assessment done by the local revenue staff viz. *Muqaddams* and *Chaudharies* of the villages and the *Parganas Shiqdar*, who in this respect were responsible to the *Amin* of the area. On assignment , he was entrusted with the ledger of detailed total revenue (*Dhol Jama*) of his *Jagir* certified by the higher *Subah* officers.[6]

For the land revenue collection, a Jagirdar commanded two-fold staff, the official villages of the *Pargana* revenue machinery and his personal revenue staff. The village and the *Pargana* officials discharged their duties of revenue collection irrespective of the *Khalsa* or the *Jagir* administration.[7] In case of a small assignment, the Patwaries, the *Chaudharies* and the *Zamindars* and in case of a large assignment covering the whole *Pargana*, the *Shiqdar* and his whole *Pargana* staff worked for the *Jagirdar* for the land revenue collection.[8]

Similarly, when a full *Sarkar* or at times the whole *Subah* was assigned to a Prince, the Royal machinery of the territory under his assignment worked in coordination with him, but was never considered as a part of his personal staff. In case of need, apart from his claim of getting support from the *Faujdar* of the Division, he could as well appeal for additional help to *Diwan-i-Subah* but in the latter case he had to pay for the expenses of the provincial contingents despatched by the *Diwan* for his help.[9] At times, as an emergency measure, a *Jagirdar* could entrust his entire *Jagir* to the *Subha* authorities for its administration during the period of his absence. In such a case, the revenues of his *Jagir* would be collected from the official state agency as if it were a part of the *Khalsa* and the Jagirdar could claim the stipulated amount as revenues from the *Diwan* of the *Subah.*[10]

Apart from the Government official machinery, a *Jagirdar* possessed his own revenue staff for the management of his *Jagir*. High *Mansabdars*, especially the Princes, owning large assignments of revenues of various *Parganas*, appointed a high revenue officer of the rank of *Diwan* to manage the financial matters of their *Jagirs.*[11] It seems that such *Diwans* attached to the *Jagirs* of the high ranking *Mansabdars* were State servants holding even a *Mansab* and were specially deputed with the Prince or high Mansabdars for the management of their *Jagirs.*[12] Even their appointment was made by the Central Government though, of course, with the consent of the *Jagirdars* with whom they were attached.[13]

As most of the *Jagirdars* were absentee officers posted at different places than their assignments, they had their own touring agents (*Gumashtas*), who would pass on the detailed periodical reports on the affairs of the collection and the arrears of the revenues in different villages and the conduct of the revenue officials of the *Jagirdar* posted in a *Pargana.*[14] Besides this, the *Jagirdar* had personal revenue staff posted in every *Pargana*. The official documents put the *Jagirdar's* revenue officials under the general designation of either *Gumashta*[15] or *Mutsaddi.*[16] Most appropriately, the representative revenue of the *Jagir* was known as *Amil* of the *Jagirdar* or simply as an *Amil* as distinct from the *Amil* of the *Khlasa* or the *Karori*. He is designated as such throughout the Mughal age. An *Amil* of a *Jagirdar* was a counterpart of a *Karori* in the *Khalsa* administration and, as such, was the Revenue Collector of the *Jagir* land. He had to execute a bond for the collection of the land revenue within a specified period and for the proper discharge of his duties.[18] In case of an assignment of the full *Pargana* with the *Jagirdar*, the *Amil* possessed higher rank than the *Shiqdar*, who, along with his entire *Pargana* revenue staff, worked under the former for the collection of revenues.[19] He could hold his court wherein the *Shiqdars, Thanedars, Chaudharies* and the

Muqaddams could be summoned for making appropriate arrangements for the collection of the revenue. Even in an assignment of small *Jagirs* comprising of few villages in a *Paragana*, the Revenue Collector of the *Jagirdar* was designated as *Amil*.[21] The *Amil* of the *Jagirdar* had his own staff of various agents for the collection of revenues, who were all designated by the general permission of *Gumashtas*.[22] The *Amil* and his *Gumashtas* had to attest his income ledger of the *Jagir* which was submitted to them for inspection duly signed by the *Chaudharies, Qanungos* and the *Thanedars* of their *Jagir* territory. The *Amil* also maintained his contingents of solidiers of *Sawars* and *Paidas* (known as *Seh Bandi*), who were earmarked for different places under the supervision of a *Gumashta* for the revenue collection.[23] The *Amil* was also in direct contact with the *Chaudharies, Qanungos* and *Muqaddams* of the villages for the realisation of the revenues.[24]

The *Amil* and his staff were appointed and removed by the *Jagirdar* and were directly responsible to the latter. The *Jagirdar* could take action against them for any mis-conduct or mis-appropriation of money.[25] Usually, an 'with any affliation in the assigned territory of his *Jagirdar* was not appointed as he could easily connive with the *Zamindars* and the local officials against the interests of his own *Jagirdar*. In case the revenue collection was done in kind, the *Amil* had to arrange for the deposit and the transport of the grain to the nearest market and after a careful study of the market prices had to arrange for the sale of the corn at reasonable rates.[26] After the collections were made in cash or when the sale proceeds of the corn taken in kind were effected, he had to forward the amounts to the *Jagirdar*.[27] An *Amil* of a big *Jagirdar* had to despatch copies of all the documents relating to the periodical prices, the collection of revenue, the arrears, the expenditure on the contigent maintained for the collection for the collection of revenue (*Seh Bandi*) and the other revenue staff and as well to submit a report on the condition of the *ryots*.[28] The *Amil* had to despatch a comprehensive report on the state of agriculture in the *Jagir* territory relating to the estimated revenue for either of the crops-*Kharif* and *Rabi*, the assessment made in each crop, the areas under crops in each season for every village, the increase in produce against the last years, details of crops where means of irrigation were available, report on the rainfall and consequent production of the *Kharif* crop, the sale of the corn and the amount realised from all the village, the lands given in *Ijara* if any, and the amount realised.[29] The *Amil* of a big *Jagirdar* could even directly correspond with the *Diwan-i-Subah* relating to affairs and difficulties in the administration of the *Jagir* and could seek his help, if needed.[30]

For the expenditure involved in the revenue collection the *Jagirdar* paid the remunerations of his own personal staff viz, the *Amil, Gumashtas* and the contingent maintained for it. The remunerations of the village officials like *Muqaddams, Patwaris*, paid *Surveyors*, the *Chaudharies* and the *Zamindars* were not a liability on his budget as all those officials were entitled to either rent free grant or percentage in the collections made. The *Jagirdar* was always made an assignment on the basis of *Hale-i-Hasil* (actual *Hasil*), which already took cognizance of these prerequisites.

Footnotes

1. A.N. Br. M.Add. 27, 247 fol 332a Ms. pp. 92-110, 107-108, 123-128; T.J. Ms. Rampur p. 17, BGII. tr. Borah, pp. 518, 523-24.
2. A.N. Br. Add. 27, 247, Fol. 332a.
3. *Ibid.*
4. *The English Factories* (1646-50) pp. 299-301 vide Richard, Do vide the Richard, Danidge and Thomas Andrews of the Agra, President and Council at Sarat, Feb. 15, 1650 A.D. It mentions the robbery of a caravan of the E.I. Co. which lead to a petition by the latter to the Royal Court. The Royal orders were issued to the *Jagirdar* that if the goods were not restored, he had "to make good their value". The scholars hitherto have not understood the nature of the executive powers of the *Jagirdar*. Both Dr. Satish Chandra (vide *Party and Politics*, p. 27 and Dr. Saran (vide *Provincial Government*, p. 108) are not correct in their statement that the *Jagirdars* had no administrative powers.
5. B.G., B.N. Paris, fol. 145b; R.A.J. *Maharaja's Letters* Reg. No. 1123 dated A.H. 1111/1700 A.D. also category no. 4 Reg. No. 405 dated 19th *Jamada* I.A.H. 1117/1705 A.D.
6. S.D.S.R. pp. 21, 23, 147, 158, 176. Also R.A.J. *Yakil Report* from Kesho Rai to Maharaj Bishen Singh, Camp Bijapur, dated 19th *Rajab*, 31st R.Y.1688 gives details of the basic revenue (Fords of Dhole), which were sanctioned by Emperor Aurangzeb.
7. The *Chaudharies, Qanungos* and other officials were duty bound to help the *Amil* of the *Jagir* in the land revenue realisation. See details S.D.S.R., pp. 21, 23, 147, 150, 158; R.A.J. *Akhbarat, Waqai* Othal *Subah* Ujjain, Reg. No. 630 dated 13th *Jamada* II, 49th R.Y.A.H. 1117/21st September 1705 A.D.; Also report of Ganga Ram *Waqai Nawis* dated 14th *Jamada* II; A.H. 1117/ 22nd September 1705 A.D.

8 Ms pp. 18, 22; *Maqtubat-Khan Jahan* fol. 63A *Matin-i-Insha.*, fols 6b-7a; R.A.J. *Akhbarat, Waqai Nigar's* Report of *Pargana* Othal Reg NO. 679 dated 15 *Jamada* I.A.H. 1117/23rd September 1705; also *Waqai Pargana Othal* Reg No. 654 dated 12th Rabi 2nd; 49th R.Y.A.H. 1117, 1705 AD; also see Fn 7.

9. R.A.J., *Misc. Pers. Documents* Reg No. 419 dated 12th *Rajab* 49th R.Y. A.H. 1117/1705 A.D. narrates bond or (*Muchalka*) executed by the *Amil* of the *Jagirdar* for standing stipulated amount as expenses of the contingent to be despatched by *Diwan-i-Subah.*
10. B.G.II, Tr. Borah, p. 673 narrates that Rs. 30,000/- were assigned to Shitab Khan by Khan Fath Jang for the *Rabi* crop of *Pargana* Khuntagat (Kitch, *Subah* Bengal) while the former was posted away for military operation. Later on, Shitab Khan made a claim of the above amount from Mir Safi, the *Diwan* of Kutch and was given a draft (*sanad*) for the realisation of the

money. Also R.A.J. *Akhbarat* dated 9th *Rajab*, 9th R.Y. (Aurangzeb) quotes a petition from Raj Ali Khan that he had been posted out to Kabul and Bayawar while his *Jagir* was in Lahor. Thereupon, the Emperor ordered that the *Diwan* of *Subah* Lahor should realise the revenue of his *Jagir* and hand over to the assignee.

11. B.G.I tr. Borah pp. 12-13, 203 mentions Muhammed Murad, the *Diwan* and Personal Assistant of Ihtiman Khan. The *Diwan* appointed Revenue Collectors in different places for the collection of revenue and administration of the *Jagir Parganas* assigned in Bengal and Orissa. Also, *Ibid*, II, pp. 625, 627, 676. Mirza Nathan appointed his own *Diwan*, Balabhadra for the administration of his *Jagirs*; also see B.G. II. p.747 which mentions Ray Jawahar Mal Dass, the *Diwan* to Ibrahim Khan Fath Jang; Also B.G. I p. 205 clearly mentions Sheikh Bhikam as personal *Diwan* of Islam Khan, the Governor of Bengal, whereas the official *Diwan* of the *Subah* was Mutqid Khan; Also *Qazwini*, Ms. Rampur p. 310. Also *The English Factories* (1651-54) pp. 51, 112, which mention the *Diwan* of Prince Dara Shikoh and Princess Jahan Ara respectively. Also R.A.J. *Akhbarat* Reg No. 1433/1 dated 2nd Rabi I, 23rd R.Y. (Aurangzeb) mentions Rehmat Khan as the *Diwan* of Prince Shah Alam.

12. *Qazwini*, Ms. Rampur mentions that during the first regnal year of Shahjahan, Hakim Jamadi Kashi with a *Mansab* of 800 *Zat* and 200 *Sawars* was appointment as the *Diwan* of Nawab Mohd Alayi. Also R.A.J. *Akhbarat* vide Fn. 10.

13. R.A.J. *Vakil Report* No. 25/46 dated 20th *Muharram*, 25th R.Y. A.H. 1093/1681 A.D. *Akhbarat* Reg. NO. 44/241 dated 25th *Jamada* I, 44 regnal Year (Aurangzeb).

14. *Maktubat-i-Khan Jahan*, Br. M. Fol 63-64, Riazul Vidad, *Letters of Azad Bakshi to various Jagirdars*, Br. N.O.R. 1725, fols 3b, 4a, 11a, 24b.

15. A.N., BG/M, Add 27, 427, fol 232a; S.D.S.R. pp. 18, 21, 23, *Gumashta* meant an agent. The term was used as much for the representatives of other high officials as for the *Amil* of the *Jagirdar*. (Vide Akbar's *Farman* for remission of *Zakat* dated A.H. 999/1587 AD., Mirat I, pp. 171-72). In fact, the *Gumashta* of a *Jagirdar* in a *Pargana* was the same official as to *Amil* of the *Jagridar*.

16. Jahangir uses the term as '*Mutsaddis* of *Khalsa* and *Jagirdars*' vide T.J. Ms. Rampur, p.10 Also BGII tr. Borah, p. 676 mentions *Mutsaddis* as *Amils* of the *Jagridars*, The designation *Mutsaddi* meant a revenue officials and was used in the general sense as much for the Government officers as for an *Amil* of a *Jagirdar* though in the official documents the latter use was extremely rare.

17. A.N. Br. M. Add 27, 247 fols 53b, *Makutabat-i-Khan Jahan*, Br. M, fols 63a-b, *Mirat* I, p. 304.

18. R.A.J. *Misc. Pers Documents*, Reg No. 732 dated 26th *Jamada* I, 49th regnal year 1117 A.H./1705 A.D.

19. Ms., pp. 18, 22; RAJ. *Report of Waqai Nigar* vide Reg No. 688 dated 24th *Jamada* I 49th Regnal Year A.H. 1117/1705 A.D.; *Akhbarat, Waqai Nagar's* Report *Pargana* Othal, Reg. NO. 679 dated 15th Jamada I 49th Regnal year A.H. 1117/24th August 1705 A.D. These reports clearly show that the *Shiqdar* and the *Thandars* in a *Pargana* worked in cooperation with the *Amil* of the *Jagirdar*.

20. R.A.J. *Akhbarat, Waqai Pargana* Othal Reg. No. 630 dated 13th Jamada II 49th Regnal Year A.H. 1117/21st September 1705 A.D.; also dated 14th Jamada II A.H. 1117; also report of the *Waqai Nagars* vide nos 21.

21. R.A.J. *Akhbarat Waqai Pargana* Othal Reg. No. 630 dated 13th Jamada II 49th R.Y. A.H. 1117, 21st September 1705; also 14th Jamada II, dated 1117 A.D., Report of the *Ganga Rama Waqai Nawis*; Also *Waqai Pargana* Othal, Reg. No. 654 dated 12th Rabi II 49th R.Y. A.H. 1117/1705 A.D.

22. Ms. B.N. Paris Suppl. Persian 2052 comprising archival letters of Aurangzeb's reign. See letters Nos. 1 & 3 from the *Pargana* Othal Reg No. 654, dated 2nd Rabi II 49th R.Y. A.H. 1117/23rd July 1705 A.D.

23. R.A.J. uncatalogued *Seh Bandi Pargana* documents of Aurangzeb's reign.

24. R.A.J. *Waqai Pargana* Othal Reg. No. 654 dated 12th *Rabi* 49th R.Y. A.H. 1117/1705 A.D.

25. B.GII tr. Borah, p.663 in case of misappropriation of money by *Aqataqi*, the *Amil* Qulij Khan, who took the stringent measures of impressing the *Amil* and his staff and took the entire family of the *Amil* in hostage before the accounts were cleared; also R.A.J. *Misc. Pers. Document* NO. 2497, undated (Auranzeb's reign) quotes the dismissal of an *Amil* b, the *Jagirdar*.

26. *Maktubat-i-Khan Jahan*, fols 54a-55b, 63a-b.

27. *Ibid.*

28. R.A.J. *Misc. Pers. Documents, Jama Wasil Baqi Documents* Reg. No. 1117 dated 1100 Fasli/1688 A.D. of the villages of *Pargana* Malavai Sarkar Kara, *Subah* Akhrabad in the *Jagir* of Maharaja of Amber; also *Misc. Pers. Documents,* reg No. 1157 dated 1100 Fasli/1688 A.D. of *Pargana* Jalani in the *Jagir* of Mirza Mohmmed Jan Beg.

29. R.A.J. Category no. 2 Case no. 93, dated A.H. 1091 submits a detailed report to the *Diwan* relating the working of the *Jagir* of Maharaja of Amber for the *Parganas* in *Subah* Ujjain; also *Misc. Pers. Documents* Reg. No. 1576 dated 7th Farrakhi Regnal Year; A.H. 1130/1718 A.D.; Also Reg. No. 1577 dated A.H. 1131.

30 R.A.J. Misc. 419 dated 12th Rajab, 49th R.Y. A.H. 1117/1705 A.D.

3

Fiscal Rights and Obligations of Jagirdar

A *Jagirdar* was entitled to the assigned land revenue and a fixed share in the *sair* (miscellaneous) of the villages and *Mahals* under assignment. The assignment was made for the *Hasil* calculated after the deduction of the collection charges by the local officials, i.e. *Muqaddams, Chaudharies* and *Patwaries* etc. of village or a *Pargana* which was free from any assignment of *al-tamgha Inam*, and *Madad-i-Maash*, but nobody was known as *Sair-i-Hasil*.[1] So unless assigned a *Sair-i-Hasil* territory, the assignee's claim on the revenues for his salary was always made after having reckoned the revenues of the *Inams* and *Madad-i-Maash* assignment made in the villages or the *Parganas* being assigned to the *Jagirdar* in *Tankhwah Jagir*. Of course, if the *Jagirdar* was not satisfied with the expected *Hasil* of the assignment made, he could get the villages re-surveyed and re-assessed.[2]

At times, a *Jagirdar* could refuse a particular assignment on any legitimate ground and the proposed assignment could be made to another person.[3] An assignee of *Tankhwah Jagir* was not expected to tamper with the revenues occurring to the assignees of the maintenance grants.[4]

For the purposes of exactions of the revenues, the *Jagirdars* were bound by the imperial regulations. Todar Mal's 27th years revenue regulations ordering the collections to be made strictly in accordance with the schedule code (*Dastur-ul-amal*) were as much binding on the *Jagirdars* and their *Amils* as for the *Khalsa* administration.[5] The surveyors of land and the agents of collection of land revenue (*Muqaddams* and *Chaudharies*) were also warned against any connivance with the *Amils* for any undue realisation from the *ryots*. In case of any unauthorized realization, the amount was to be reimbursed to the credit of the cultivators at the next crop and the defaulters were to be punished.[6] A Royal decree for the remission of a portion of land revenue or the abolition of a cess or custom duty was equally operative in the *Khalsa* and the *Jagir* territories. For the collection of the revenues in cash, the *Jagirdar* was to apply the Royal currency regulations for deduction charges on the old coins.[7] As for the *Khalsa* lands, the *Jagirdar* was, of course, entitled to the perquisites of the chivalry (*Sawar*) and footmen (*Paiyada*) employed for the actual collection of the revenues.[8] Apart from it, the agents of the *Jagirdars* were strictuly forbidden to collect any illegal cesses and the *Muqaddams* and *Chaudharies* were strictly enjoined not to make any unauthorised payment to them.[9]

The *Jagirdars* were expected to increase the agricultural produce especially of the high grade crops (*Jins-i-Amil*) and to look after the welfare of the *ryots* and the *Madad-i-Maash* assignments in their areas.[10] The *Jagirdars* were expected to upkeep the existing irrigation channels in their areas and to extend further such irrigating facilities in their territories.[11] In accordance with the practice of the *Khalsa* land, the *Jagirdar* had to advance *Taqawi* loans to the cultivators and afford them full remissions in land revenue sanctioned by the State in case of failure of crops or natural calamity. For any remissions granted to the cultivators, they were to be given a reduction (*Takhfif*) from their sanctionhed salary in lieu of which they were compensated either in cash from the treasury or an additional assignment from the *Paibaqi* lands. In short, all the *Khalsa* rules and regulation for advance of money to the cultivators and the remissions afforded to them in adverse circumstances were also assigned on the *Jagir* administration.

It seems that the *Jagirdar* of a large assignment was competent to effect changes in the existing mode of assessment in his area provided the method of assessment was within the Imperial regulations and the assessment of revenue was done by the local revenue assessment officials. But any change in the method of assessment had to be effected with the consent of the *ryots* or else it would incur strong resentment on the part of the latter.[12] Usually, the existing regional practice of mode of assessment was followed.

It is clear from the documents of the reign of Shahjahan and Aurangzeb that for the collection of the revenues, a *Jagridar* could pass on his assignment or a portion thereof on *Ijara* to a *Mustajir* on stipulated terms for a fixed term of period at his discretion. At times, a *Jagirdar* could undertake the collection of the *Paibaqi* lands on the condition of charging 1/3rd of the revenues. Sometimes the State of its own preferred to pass on some of the *Paibaqi Mahals*, especially in a disturbed area to a big *Jagirdar* for the collection of the revenues on similar conditions.[13]

Apart from the financial aspect of the *Jagir* administration, a *Jagirdar* owed certain socio-religious obligations. Jahangir ordered that like the

Khalsa Amils, a *Jagirdar* could construct inns and mosques in his area as to make it conducive to populous growth, Similarly, in the big cities he should construct hospitals for the ailing persons for which the cost of construction would be defrayed by the State exchequer.[14]

Footnotes

1. Ms. Or. Fol. 306, fol 2b. Dr. Satish Chandra's definition of *Sair-i-Hasil* as 'productive and easily manageable *Jagir*' is wrong (vide *Party and Politics at the Mughal Court*, Introduction p. xxiii) of *Sair-i-Hasil* area could be retained in the *Khalsa* or given in *Tankhwah Jagir* to an assignee.
2. *Baharistan-i-Ghaibi*, tr. Borah II, Gauhati, 1936, p. 741. Tajpur Purnea in the newly conquered territories of Bengal was assigned to Shri Khan Fathe-Jang in lieu of his salary but the latter refused to accept it as he had doubts as to the correct assessment of the revenue. Thereupon, Jahangir issued a *Farman* to the effect "it has been represented that Shri Khan would accept that assignment if a correct statement of the revenues of those two places were made by a trustworthy officer." The *Farman* orders Shitah Kha, " to make a thorough inquiry into conditions of the *ryots* of those two *Mahals*, so that neither the *ryots* nor the *Jagirdar* may be put to hardship nor the Imperial revenues fall short, and then you are bound to send a report to the court." Thereupon, full enquiries were made by Yara Khan along with Khwaja Todar Mal and correct estimate of the revenues of the *Parganas* were made with the consent of the *ryots*, signatures of the *Quanungos* and the deed of agreement of the *Chaudharies*, which was duly verified by the agents of Shir Khan, the assignee before acceptance.
3. *Ibid*, p.776. *Pargana* Tajpur was ascertained Rs. 120,000 and was assigned to Shir Khan in lieu of his salary for 6 months but the latter did not accept it. Ultimately, after the reluctance on the part of various other persons was assigned to Sayd Shajaat Khan.
4. Ms. pp. 191-93.
5. A.N. Br. M.27, 247, Fol. 331 b
6. *Ibid.*
7. A.N. Br. M27, 247, fol 332b.
8. R.A.J. *Akhbarat*, Reg. No. 635, *Waqai Report of Pargana Othal, Sarkar* Ujjain, *Subah* Malwa, dated 22nd *Jamada* 2nd, 49th R.Y. A.H. 1113/1701 A.D. quotes a bond (*Muchalka*) given by the *Muqaddam* Mohan and Udhai Sen *Thanedar* for the payment to the *Sawar* and *Paiyada*.
9. *Selected Documents of Shah Jahan's Reign, daftar-i-Diwanni*, Hyderabad, Deccan, 1950, pp. 189-90.
10. R.A.J. *Akhbarat Farman, Amil* and *Mutsadhis* of the Empire dated A.H. 990/1578AD vide *Insha-i-Illami* Ms. Orient, Oct., 1146 Berlin, Fols 42a-42b, Akbar's *Farman* to Shahbaz Khan, Governor of Malwa vide Ms. Berlin fol. 46A; also S.D.S. pp. 21, 23.
11. Ms. pp. 13, 17-18.
12. Fbr Akbar's reign, see T.M. pp. 246-46. For Shahjahan's reign, see M.S. pp. 13-14, 51, 101, 121, 145-46, 154-155.
13. R.A.J. *Vakil Report* dated 19th *Rajab* 31st R.Y. (Aurangzeb). Also category No. 4, Reg. NO. 2572 dated 15th *Shaban* A.H. 1123.
14. *Tuzuk-i-Jahangiri*, Ms. Rampur, pp. 9-10.

4

Transfer of Jagir

The transfer of an assignment of *Tankhwah Jagir* was an established principle throughout the Mughal age.[1] The only exception was the *Watan Jagir* held by a *Zamindar* in his *Zamindari*.[2] Already known to the Timuride administration, the Mughal State viewed the problem from its own angle of stability and integrity of the Empire on the one hand and interests of the subjects on the other. It obviated the dangers of any permanent vested landed interests on the part of the bureaucrats and served as a great deterrent to high *Mansabdars* with large assignments for establishing an 'Imperio in Imperium'[3] On the contrary, the lure of more productive and administratively convenient *Mahals* for assignment always kept even the higher *Mansabdars* in servility and dependence upon the State.[4] At the same time, a mis-managed assignment of an oppressive *Jagirdar* could be easily transferred which, in fact, was basic idea of a transferable *Jagir*.[5] Thus, as a matter of practice, the Mughal Government did not allow a *Jagirdar* to keep a particular assignment for a long time. There was no fixed tenure and any assignment could be transferred any time at the discretion of the monarch. All the same, on an average, a *Jagirdar* could retain his *Jagir* from 3 to 7 years.[6]

How a person was assigned a particular *Jagir* depended on the administrative convenience of the Revenue Ministry and the capability of the assignee to manage it.[7] The Revenue Ministry was by no means bound to make an assignment in or around the assignee's posting and made assignments even regardless of Provincial boundaries.[8] Of course, if a *Mansabdar* was posted in a particular Province on military grants, he was assigned *Jagir* at the same place. As such, *Mansabdars* serving in the Deccan were usually assigned *Jagirs* over there.[9] Evey the *Zamindars-Mansabdars* (*Rajas*) etc., apart from their *Watan Mahal* could hold *Jagirs* both in North India and the Deccan.[10] Aurangzeb as Prince protested against the practice of assignees' *Jagirs* to the officers serving in the Deccan essentially in Deccan territories[11], but as a monarch in 1694 A.D., he ordered that only those persons serving there may be assigned *Jagirs* in the Deecan.[12] Usually, a *Faujdar* would be assigned *Jagir* at the place of his posting [13] though at times his assignment could be at a different place of his posting.[14] Ordinarily, a *Faujdar* was given assignment of a recalcitrant (*Zur Talb*) area of the same province of his posting.[15] The Revenue Ministry paid due consideration to the capability of an assignee for the realisation of the revenues and the management of the area.[16] As a matter of rule, the high ranking *Mansabdars* were to be made assignments at scattered places in different types of areas, viz. docile and revenue paying (*Rayta* or *Rayati*), seditious (*Zur Talb*), average i.e. partly revenue pay and partly seditious (*Mahmur* or *Ausat*), desolate with much less revenues (*Warian*)[17].

Financial Adjustment in Revenues on Account of Jagir Transfers

As the Muslim conquest in India took place during *Kharif* season, the beginning of the year was taken from *Kharif* crop. Usually, as a matter of practice, fresh appointment to an assignment or transfer to a new *Jagir* was made either from the beginning of the *Kharif* crop[18] or during any of the months following in the *Kharif* season.[19] But on grants of administrative expediency transfers were also effected from the beginning or during the *Rabi* seaons.[20] The *Jagirdar* was entitled to full revenue for the *Kharif* crop if posted at the beginning of the season, but if he were posted in the midst of the season, he could claim revenues only in accordance with the *Jagir* month-schedule. Of the total collections made, apart from his own share of the revenues, he had to return the balance to the State exchequer as *Baz Yaft*. He could undertake to pay this amount as *Mutalba* to the state after full realisations were made. When a *Jagir* was transferred in the midst of a season and was not attached to the *Khalsa* but given to a new assignee, the new assignee was not entitled to any realisation made so far and would be compensated from the exchequer in accordance with the month scale schedule. At the same time, the total realisations were to be shared between an old assignee and the State according to the schedule. For the months already due for his salary, he would be compensated from the state exchequer.[21] But if an assignee was posted out in the midst of the season before the realisations were effected, he was compensated in cash from the State treasury in accordance with the schedule.[22] As a matter of rule, when an assignee was transferred and the *Jagir* was given to the another one, the date of grant was numbered from the date of original order or transfer regardless of the possession taken later on. As such, the new assignee was entitled to the revenue of that *Jagir* from the date of appointment.[23] Though actually the *Rabi* and the *Kharif* seasons were not of the equal value, officially they were put in equal in value for the purposes of transfer. As such, a *Jagirdar* ordinarily preferred to be posted or transferred during the *Kharif* season.[24] Even when on grants of administrative expediency, a *Jagirdar* was posted either at the beginning or during the *Rabi* seasons, he was always anxious to enjoy the revenues of the next *Kharif* crop.[25]

Footnotes

1. This is evident from all the chronicle accounts of the foreign travellers and the revenue literature from Akbar to Aurangzeb. See A.N. II, pp. 332-33, *Insha-i_Allami*, Ms. Oct. 1140, Berlin, fol. 46b, Bernier, pp. 208, 227; De Laet, 94-95.

2. Some other exceptions could also be made as Aurangzeb conceded the *Jagir* of *Pargana* Shon to Begum Zeenat-ul-Nisa on permanent basis vide *Akhbarat* dated 18th Rabi II, 11th R.Y. 5th Sept 1669 A.D.

3. At times, the assignment to the Princes was done for the entire Province and other high *Mansabdars* were assigned a full *Sarkar* division or even more territory. *Mahazar-i-Shahjahani*, pp. 89-193 quotes the full *Sarkar* of Sehwar *Subah* Thatta comprising 11 *Parganas* always assigned to one *Jagirdar* right from Akbar's to Shahjahan's periods. *Mirat* I. p. 286 puts the whole *Sarkar* of Surat with the *Faujdar* of Surat.

4. *Maktib-i-Allami*, N.A.I. p.15. The documents of Aurangzeb reign are replete with petitions from the *Faujdars* for the transfer and better assignments. See R.A.J. *Vakil Reports*, Reg. No. 390/297 datd 29th *Zul-quda*, 35th R.Y. A.H. 1102/14th August 1691 A.D., Reg. No. 936/609, 4th *Ramzan*, A.H. 1105/9th Feb 1694.

5. Akbar's *Farman* of Nizamuddin Shahbaz Khan, the Governor of Malwa directs that any assignee who does not administer in accordance with the rules and regulations of the State, his *Jagir* may be transferred. Thereafter, it may be intimated to the Royal Court so that some other benevolent and trustworthy persons may be appointed therein as the administration of the State rests on this very principle. Vide Akbar's *Farman* to Shahbaz Khan, Governor of Malwa, dated A.H. 990/1578 A.D. quoted in *Makabat-i-Allami*, N.A.I. p. 105; *Insha-i-Allami*, Ms. Orient, Oct 1140 Fol. 46b. Timur established a rule that an *Amir* may be in the first instance given in assignment for 3 years and thereafter on inspection if it was found that the *ryots* were happy and the territory was prosperous, *Jagir* may be renewed or else should be reverted to *Khalsa* and the *Jagirdar* should not be given an assignment for the next 3 years vide *Malfuzat-i-Timuri*, Ms. Berlin fol 66b.

6. William Hawkins in Jahangir's reign put the shortest period of transfer at 6 months and longest at 6 years. Vide *Early Travels*, pp. 83, 91, 93, 114. *Mahazar Shahjahani* vide pp. 89-193 narrates the tenures of 15 *Jagirs* in the *Sarkar* of Sehwan from the day of his conquest under Akbar to 1042 A.H./1630 A.D. Of these, it states that Bakhtayar Beg, the first *Jagirdar* after conquest in Akbar's reign, held assignment for 7 years (*Ibid* p.101); Pir Gulam held *Jagir* under Akbar and Jahangir twice for 6 years each (*Ibid* pp. 108-114, 121). Various *Jagirdars* held *Jagirs* for shorter durations. For Aurangzeb's reign, *Vakil Report* Reg. No. 1265/95 dated 4th Jamada I, 50th R.Y., A.H. 1118/13th August 1706 A.D. mentioned the duration period of Man Singh's *Jagir* in *Pargana* Banhar (*Panhar*) *Subah* Akbarabad for 6 to 7 years

7. R.A.J. *Vakil Report* Reg. No. 936/609 4th *Ramzan* 38th R.Y.A.H. 1105/19th April 1694 records a letter from the *Vakil* to the *Maharaja* for taking *Pargana* Kol under his administration with the help of the *Diwan* of the *Subah* because the *Maharaja* could manage affairs of the *Pargana* better than Atiq Ullah, the present assignee, and could get more revenues even on the old rates.

8. For regulations on contingents of the *Mansabdars* for having been posted at different places, see details *Khulasatu-s Siyaq*, Ad 1703 No. A.I., ff 89a-90a; also Lahori, II, pp. 506-7.

9. S.D.S.R. pp. 17, 50

10 *Ibid*, pp. 175-77.

11. *Adab-i-Alamgiri*, MS. Aligh, fols 18-b-19a, 25b, 40a-40b, 43a; Ms printed text pp. 56-58.

12. R.A.J. *Akhbarat* 38 R.Y.

13. *Maasir-i-Jahangiri*, Ms. No. 563, Aligh, fol 53a; also *Mirat* I p.286

14. *Ibid*, fol. 141b; also *Vakil Report* Reg. No. 369/239 28th *Shaban* A.H. 1101/ 17th May 1690 A.D.

15. *Mirat*, Suppl. pp. 205-6.

16. See Emperor Farrkh Sayar's Order vide *Mirat* I pp. 341, 343, 359.

17. *Siyaqnama* Ms. Hydbd, fol 14b. According to 18th Century M.s *Hidayat-al-Qawaid*, (Ms. Aligh. Fol 8a, copy of Sh. Abdur Rashid p.13) *Naiimas* had to be assigned 1/4th of the amount in seditious area and ¾ th the average, *Diwan* and *Bakhshi* etc; ½ in excellent revenue paying and the small *Jagirdars* were to be given 1/4th in average and ¾ in revenue paying. It seems that such a principle had been followed in the earlier reigns too.

18. SN Hydbd, fol 5b

19 *Ibid.* 64, 77, 175; *Vakil Report* No. 390/279 datd 29th Zul-quda A.H. 1102/ 14th August 1691 A.,D.

20. *Akhbarat* first of *Jamada* I, 24th R.Y. *Letters to the Maharaja*, Reg. No. 887, 40th R.Y. A.H. 1107/1695 A.D.

21. R.A.J. *Akhbarat* No. 1290 dated 11th Rabi I, 10th R.Y. (Aurangzeb); also Reg. No. 1349 dated 23rd *Shawwal* 10th R.Y. (*Ibid*).

22 S.D.S.R. pp. 77-78.

23 *Vakil Report*, reg. no. 1096/800 dated 17th *Safar* 48th R.Y., A.H. 1116/10th June 1704 quotes the rule in details.

24. R.A.J. *Akhbarat* No. 1329, dated 21st Rabi II 10th R.Y. quotes a petition submitted by Ala Vari Khan that in *Subah* Orissa, the *Kharif* crop was much in abundance whereas the *Rabi* crop was much less in produce and *Hasil* with a request to assign the *Jagir* with effect from the *Kharif* crop. But the Emperor rejected the petition that henceforth the *Rabi* and *Kharif* crops should be taken at equal value. It seems that before this order, they were recknoed at an unequal value.

25 R.A.J. *Akhbarat*, first of *Jamada* I 24th R.Y. quotes a petition from the *Vakil* of Shah Quli Khan that the latter was given assignment of the *Parganas* in the mid of the *Rabi* season and requests that he be allowed to enjoy the assignment as to cover the next *Khari* crop.

5

Checks on the Authority of the Jagirdars

To ensure the application of the Imperial regulations in the *Jagir* administration and to safeguard the interests of the *ryot* against any exploitation or harshness on the part of the *Jagirdar* and his *Amils*, the Mughal State provided a number of checks upon him.

(i) The Imperial Control

The Emperor in the Central Ministry exercised the vigilant control over the working of the *Jagir* system. The very institution of the transfer of *Jagirdars* was intended to be a check against the mis-management of the *Jagir*.[1] A report against the *Jagirdar* lodged either by the Provincial Government or the *ryot* was liable to get him transferred. The *Jagirdar* was always enjoined to keep the *ryots* happy[2] and the retention of a good *Mahal* in *Jagir* for a long period or its restoration after some time[3] or the assignment of a *Tankhwah Jagir* of a *Zamindar-Mansabdar* near his own *Watan Mahal* depended essentially on the satisfaction of the *ryots*.[4] On persistent complaints for gross negligence of the management of his *Jagir*, his *Jagir* was confiscated and he was put as *Naqdi Mansabdar*.[5] On any serious complaint against an *Amil* of a *Jagirdar*, the Central Government could directly send orders to the latter reprimanding him and send a copy of the same to the *Jagirdar* concerned.[6] The Emperor closely watched the activities of the big *Jagridars* and in case of any dereliction would often reprimand them for running their *Jagir* administration properly.[7]

The Central Government could always summon accounts of a *Jagirdar* of any *Pargana* Division though the *Jagirdar* may have passed on the *Pargana* to an *Ijaradar* for the realisation of the revenue. Whenever the Government liked, it would send a Central *Amin* for scrutinizing all the documents of the realisations of the *Jagirdar* and the *Ijardar*.[8] In case a big *Jagirdar* mis-behaved or mis-managed the *Parganas*, his *Vakil* was at once summoned by the Central Government for explanation.[9]

(ii) Though the local village in *Pargana* officials were required to extend to a *Jagirdar* full cooperation in the realisation of the land revenue for the purpose of assessment, they worked independently of the *Jagirdar* staff and were responsible to the *Amin* of the territory.

(iii) A subordinate representative *Gumashta* of the *Waqai Nigar* was posted in every *Pargana*. The *Waqai Nigar* was in constant touch with the local officials and was entitled to attend court of the *Jagirdar* and the *Thanedar* of the area along with *Muqaddams* and the *Choudharies*.[10] He used to send daily reports on the most detailed matters of the *Jagir* administration. The *Pargana* reports of the *Waqai Nawis* comprised information on the daily activities of the *Jagirdar's Amil*, daily incidence, realisation made by the *Amil* from the *Muqaddams* of the villages and the traders, the *Amil's* attitude correspondence and daily dealings with the *Muqaddams*.[11] He would also despatch a detailed information about the proceedings of the court of the *Amil* and the *Thandedar* and the arrangement made in connection with the land revenue collections.[12] He would also note down any communication between the *Jagirdar* or his *Amil*[13] and the *Shiqdar* or the *Chaudharies*[14] and the *Muqaddams*, the dealing between the *Amil* and the *Thandar* in connection with the realisation of *Peshkash*[15], the control of the *Thandar* over the *Muqaddams* against any unauthorized payment to the *Amil*[16], the total realisation of both the *Rabi* and *Kharif* crops of the year.[17] The *Waqai Nigar* would send detailed report on the lands and assignments in different villages, the antecedents of the assignment of every *Jagirdar* and would make recommendations to the *Subah* authorities for any further adjustment in the ratio of keeping land of the villages in the *Jagir* or the *Khalsa* administration.[18] Similarly, the subordinate representative official of the *Swanih nigar* was present in all the meetings of the *Amil, Thandedars*, the *Chaudharies* and the *Muqaddams* and would despatch his independent reports to the *Swanih nigar* of the *Sarkar* Division.[19]

Check imposed by the *Subah* Administration

A *Jagirdar* did not enjoy any distinctly independent status of the provincial Government and was never vested with any absolute control over the *ryots* in his *Jagir*. Whether he himself was posted as an official in the same province of his assignment or he was posted in a different Province than that of his assignment, his *Jagir* administration was subjected to rigid control of the provincial and local administration.

(a) The *Nazim* of the Province exercised a general control over all the collectors of revenue[20] and had to look after the revenue administrative in the *Khalsa, Jagir* and the *Zamindari* lands. He was especially enjoined to see that the assignees realise the revenues only in accordance with the '*Hal-i-Hasil*' assignment and the State laws and regulations. For any dereliction from such regulations on the part of an assignee, the *Nazim* was to transfer him and to lodge a report against him to the Central Government.[21]

(b) The Provincial *Diwan* possessed powers for the management of both the *Khalsa* and the *Jagir* lands in the *Subah*. Apart from the control exercised through local officers, he himself kept direct contact with the *Jagirdars* concerning their administration in the assigned lands.[22] In case of any doubt against a *Jagirdar* for over realisation of revenues from the *ryots*, the *Diwan* had the right to summon all the records of the *Jagirdar* for the purposes of scrutiny.[23] In case a *Jagirdar* was found having concealed the excess revenues, he could be dismissed from service.[24]

(c) The *Faujdar* of a Division, whether a *Sarkar, Chakla* or a *Pargana* exercised full administrative control over both the *Khalsa* and *Jagir* lands in his jurisdiction. He would not only help a *Jagirdar* in the realisation of revenues, but had also to suppress any refractory *Jagirdar* and to ensure the application of the Imperial Regulations in the *Jagirdar* assignees.[25] At times in a large *Jagir* of a Prince, a *Faujdar* was appointed for the proper administration and the preservation of law and order.[26]

(d) The *Subah Waqai Nawis*

The *Waqai Nawis* at the *Subah* level had his subordinates spread over all the *Sarkar* and the *Parganas* in his Province, who would send regular reports to him. He watched the activities of the *Jagirdars* and had the authority to transfer any oppressive *Jagirdar*.[27] He used to send his own special *Gumashtas* for enquiry on the receipt of any complaint against a *Jagirdar*.[28] His *Gumashta* had the powers to verify any complaint after having received the original relevant documents from the *Qanungos* as to ascertain facts.[29]

(e) The *Diwan-i-Sarkar*

As the head of the revenue administration of the *Sarkar* Division, the *Diwan-i-Sarkar* had the special responsibility for superintendence over the administration of the *Jagirdars* and the well being of the *ryots* in their territories. He regularly received the assessment (*Jama*) documents from the local officials in the assigned lands and scrutinized them thoroughly.[30]

(f) The *Amin* of the *Parganas* or a *Pargana* had the jurisdiction both over the *Khalsa* and the *Jagir* lands. An *Amin* had to tour over locality in the *Jagir* lands and exercised full control for assessment over the local officials. He would essentially enforce the Imperial regulations for survey and assessment in the assigned territories.

(g) Pargana administration

(i) The *Shiqdar* of a *Pargana* was always appointed by the Central Government and even in an assigned territory, the *Jagirdar* had to accept the appointment of a *Shiqdar*, who had to keep a proper watch over the administration even in the *Jagir* lands. Full records of the lands and assignment in different villages of the *Pargana* and the documents relating to the survey, assessment, realisation and arrears, etc., both of the *Khalsa* and *Jagir* lands, were kept at the *Pargana's* headquarters. If the entire *Pargana* were in assignment, the *Shiqdar* was as much an administrator on the part of the *Jagirdar* for the realisation of the revenues as that of the Central Government so as to safeguard the interests of the *ryots* in all respects against any undue operation by the *Amil* of a *Jagirdar*.[31]

(ii) The *Thanedar* representing the *Faujdar* of the Division essentially represented the State as much for law and order as for the management of the revenue affairs. He always worked as a counter weight against any undue realisations by the *Amils* of the *Jagirdar* in his area. He kept a rigid control over the *Chaudharies* and the *Muqaddams* and got bonds (*Muchalkas*) from them so as to avoid any unauthorized payment to the *Jagirdar*.[32] Even when a full *Pargana* was given in assignment to any *Jagirdar*, the *Shiqdar* always held a higher position than the *Amil* of a *Jagirdar*. He would hold him accountable for the proper management of the *Jagir* administration so as to safeguard the interests of the *ryots*.[33]

The *Qazi*

The *Qazi* of the *Pargana* verified all documents relating to the demarcation of the boundaries (*Chaknamahs*) of the assignment and all revenue documents pertaining to the total realisation (*Tumar-Jama*) in the *Jagir*.[34] He had the special responsibility of safeguarding the interesrs of the *Madad-i-Maash* assignees in the *Tankhwah Jagir* lands.[35]

Muqaddams, Chaudharies and *Qanungos*

The *Muqaddams, Chaudharies* and *Qanungos* as the representatives of the *ryots* acted as counter-weight against any illegal realisation by the *Gumashtas* of the *Jagirdars*. For any such unauthorized realisation or undue harassment, they would lodge a complaint to the absentee *Jagirdar* and to the *Sarkar* and provincial authorities.[36] All land revenue and assessment documents remained in the custody of the *Qanungo*, who was required to produce them before the *Amin* for the purposes of next assessment.[37] The *Qanungo* had to despatch abstracts of all documents relating to the assessment realisations, remissions or arrears to the *Diwan-i-Sarkar* and the Central Government.[38] In 1692 A.D., on a report against some of the *Jagirdars* in *Subah* Gujrat that they were preventing *Desais* and *Muqaddams* from providing information about the realisation (*Hasil*) to the *Subah* officers, the Government sent special officers (*Sazavals*) to compel the *Jagirdars* for providing facilities to the local officials for the collection of the information freely and its due despatch to the higher authorites.[39]

The *ryots* of the assignees were not always docile as to submit to unauthorized realisations and oppression by the *Jagirdars'* administration. They always availed themselves of any opportunity for submitting a joint petition against *Jagirdar's* administration either to the *Subah* authorities or directly to the Central Government.[40]

*

Footnotes

1. *Makkatib-i-Allami*, NAI, p.15.
2. S.D.S.R. pp.76-77, 177.
3. *Ain* I, Blochmann, p. 328, Mirza Muzaffar Husayn, a Commander of 5000 *Mansabs*, was assigned the *Jagir* of Sambhal, "which was more than of *Qandhar*". On complaint lodged by the *ryots* against his grasping collection, his *Jagir* was confiscated and he was paid cash salary. Also R.A.J. *Akhbarat* Reg. No. 1374, dated 29th *Zul-Qada*, 10th R.Y. (Aurangzeb) quotes a procedure that before an assignment of a *Jagirdar* was extended at the same place, the *Diwan* had to certify that the *ryots* had been happy under assignee's administration.
4. R.A.J. *Vakil Report* Reg. No. 700/1418, 22nd R.Y. The report says that the *ryots* of *Pargana* Chatsu had recently complained against the Maharaja (of Amber) and that no further assignments of the *Parganas* of Malarva, Suher and Behari (near the *Watan Mahal*) was possible unless the *ryots* were satisfied with the *Maharaja's* administration.
5. *Ain* I, Blochann, p. 328; Also R.A.J. *Vakil Report* Reg. No. 928/581 dated 6th *Rajab* 37th R.Y. A.H. 1105/25th Feb 1694 A.,D. Letter from Megh Raj informs the *Maharaja* (of Amber) that owing to the mis-management in the *Jagir* of Bakhtawar Bhandoria, *Tappah* Khair was confiscated from him and transferred to the *Khalsa*. Later on it was granted in assignment to the *Maharaja*. Another report Reg. No. 195 dated 51 R.Y.A.H. 1118/1706 A.D. gives a detailed list of the *Jagirs* with revenues of various assignees which were confiscated owing to the dereliction of the *Jagirdars* from duty.
6. R.A.J. Category No. 3 Reg. No. 278 dateless (Aurangzeb's reign) Mohd. Salih Bakshi and *Waqai Nigar* of *Subah* Ajmer complained against the agents of Ram Chand, the *Mutsaddi* of the *Maharaja* of Amber with a request that a direct threatening reprimand should be sent to the *Amil* concerned.
7. *Ankam*, Ms. Rampur pp. 222/2, 223/1. On complaint against he *Jagirdars* of the *Parganas* of Thatta and Multan, Aurangzeb reprimanded the *Jagirdars* and ordered them to administrate their *Jagirs* properly. Also Adab, Ms. Rampur pp. 332-33. Aurangzeb reprimanded Mulfat Khan. Also Adab Ms Aligh fols 18a, 19b, 20a, 40a-40b. *Raqiam Kariam*, Ms. Rampur p. 95/1 quotes a letter from Aurangzeb to Prince Muam that he had received a complaint against Hasan Beg and his *Amil* Afzal Khan for mis-management of *Jagir* in *Chakla* Kora and threatened the transfer of *Jagir*. Aurangzeb also criticized his son for giving his *Jagirs* on *Ijara* and leaving them in the hands of the Iranis (Persians).
8. R.A.J. Category 4 Reg. No. 1414 dated 26th *Shaban* A.H. 1106/1690 A.D. quotes a letter from Meg Raj (*Vakil*) to the *Maharaja* (of Amber) to send an account of money realised from *Pargana* town given in *Ijara* to Safi Khan so that the *Diwan-i-Ala* may send an *Amin* for inspection and the settlement of the affairs.

9. R.A.J. *Misc. Pers Letters* Reg. No. 662 dated 2nd Jamada I, 49th R.Y. A.H. 1117/1705 A.D.

10. R.A.J. *Akhabarat* Reg. No. 688 *Waqai Nigar Pargana Othal* (*Subah* Malwa) dated 26th *Jamada* I 49th R.Y. (Aurangzeb).

11. R.A.J. *Akhbarat* Reg. No. 630 dated 13th *Jamada* I 49th R.Y. A.H. 1117/21st September, 1705 A.D. Also Reg. No. 654 dated 12th Rabi II A.H. 1117/ quotes original correspondence between the *Amil, Chaudharies* and the *Qanungos* for the realisation of the land revenues.

12. *Ibid*, Reg. No. 688 dated 24th *Jamada* I, A.H. 1117/Oct. 1705 A.D.

13. *Ibid*, Reg. No. 679, dated 15th *Jamada* I A.H. 1117, 1705 A.D.

14. *Ibid.*

15. *Ibid*, Reg. No. 635 dated 22nd *Jamada* II, 49th R.Y. A.H. 1117/1705, AD

16. *Ibid.*

17. *Ibid*, Reg. No. 656 dated 19th *Rabi* II 49th R.Y. A.H. 1117/30th July 1705 A.D.

18. R.A.J. uncatalogued *Waqai* documents dated 3rd *Ramzan* A.H. 1104, 3rd *Ramzan* A.H. 1115, 12th *Rabi* I, A.H. 1114, 25th *Rabi* II, 1115 A.H.

19. R.A.J. *Akhbarat Waqai Pargana* Othal Reg. Nos. 656, 679, Vide No. 10.

20 *Ain*, Br. M.Fols 124a, 126a; Ms Hamilton, Berlin, fol 118a.

21. *Makkatib-i-Allami*, N.A.I. p.105; Ms Oct., 1140 Berlin, fols 46a-b.

22. *Akhbarat* Reg. No. 419 dated 12th *Rajab*, 49th R.Y. 1117 A.H/1705 A.D.

23. B.G Ms. B.N. Paris, Tr. Borah II, pp. 668-69 quotes a quarrel between Shaykh Kumal, an important official and assignee and Mir Safi, the *Diwan, Bakshi,* and *Waqai Nawis* of the newly conquered territory of Kuch (*Subah* Bengal) in the reign of Jahangir. In the course of quarrel, Mr. Safi asserted, "I am the *Diwan*. It is necessary for me to have access to old records. Why then he does not submit to me the records of his revenues."

24. *Ibid*, tr. Borah II, p.671.

25. *Ain* Br. M. 6652 fols 125a-b; Ms. Hamilton, Berlin, fols 118b-119a; *Nigar Nama* Ms. N.A.I., fols 51a-b; *Insha-i-Roshan Kalam*, fols 6b, 11b.

26. R.A.J. *Akhbarat* Reg. No. 1787 dated 10th *Safar*, 24th R.Y. quotes the appointment of Mohd Tabir as the *Faujdar* and *Amin* at Kanauj, the *Jagir* of Prince Shah Alam; *Nigar Nama* Ms. Bod. Oxf, fols 76a, 77a.

27. Ms. p. 164.

28. *Ibid*, pp. 164-174, 176-77.

29. *Ibid*, pp. 176-77. Man Singh, the *Waqai Nawis* of *Subah* Thatta sent Abul Baqi to Bhakkar, who possessed a special Royal Farman for asking the documents of 10 years *Taqsin* (*Taqsim-i-Deh Sala*) and to enquire into the reasons of the desolution of the *Parganas* assigned in *Jagir*.

30. Ms. Suppl. 482 B.N. Paris fols 181a-186a; *Roznamcha-i-Baglana* (*Subah* Khandesh) dated 18th *Rabi* II, 4th R.Y. (Aurangzeb), A.H. 1072/Dec 11th, 1661 A.D., C.R.O., Hydbd. Also see details vide B.R.Grover, '*Diwan-i-Sarkar in the Mughal administration*', I.H.R.C., 1963.

31. R.A.J. *Waqai Pargana* Othal vide fn. 10.

32. R.A.J. *Akhbarat* Reg. No. 635; *Waqai Pargana* Othal from Ganga Ram *Waqai Nigar* dated 23rd Jamada II, 49th R.Y. A.H. 1117/1705 A.D., Abide Reg. No. 656 dated 19th Rabi II, 49th R.Y./30th Aug 1705 A.D. Also Reg. No. 679 dated 15th *Jamada* I, 49th R.Y.A.H. 1117/1705 A.D.

33. *Ibid.*

34. R.A.J. '*Tumar-Jama*' documents *Rabi* crop 1098 Fasli/1693 A.D.; also *Misc. Pers. Letters* Reg. No. 630 dated 26th R.Y. 1097 *Fasli*/A.H.1103/1692 A.D. are original documents duly verified by the *Chaudharies* and the *Qanungos* and stamped by a *Qazi*.

35. Ms. pp. 192-93; A.D. Reg. No. 782, 1203.

36. *Waqai Sarkar Ranthambhor*, 22nd R.Y. (Aurangzeb) p. 386; also R.A.J. *Letters to the Maharaja* Reg. No. 2188 dated 12th *Ramzan* A.H. 1129/1717 A.D. *Nigar Nama-i-Munshi*, Ms. Bod. Oxfd, fol 86b, 88a, Ms. M.A.I. fols 66b-68b.

37. M.S.Berlin fol 5a.

38. Ms. 482 B.M. Paris, fols 91a-b.

39. *Mirat* I, pp. 326-27.

40. *Mahzar-i-Shahjahani* vide p. 147 mentions that most of the religious assignees (*Imadars*) and a few representatives of the oppressed ryots traveresed all the distances from Sehwar (*Subah* Thaata) to Lahor and waited on deputation at Shahjahan's Court at Lahor and submitted their grievance to Shahjahan personally. Shahjahan appointed Shir Khwaja as an Inquiry Officer, who interviewed each of the *Imadars* and re-issued the *Mada-i-Maash Parwanas* according to the old *Chakbandis*. The Inquiry Officer also interviewed and consoled each of the *ryots* in deputation and issued an order to Shamsher Khan, the *Jagirdar*, to redress their grievance. Also, *Waqai Sarkar Ranthambhor* vide pp. 217-19 records a complaint submitted to *Subah* and the Central Authorities against Tayur Khan for harsh *Jama Bandi* and realisation of revenues. Also, *Ruqqat-i-Alamgiri*, printed text, pp. 40-41, 119.

6

The Working of the *Jagirdari* System : Its impact on the Mughal Administration and the Peasantry

With the appropriation of the major portions of the State revenues in *Tankhwah Jagirs* and *Madad-i-Maash* assignments, the greater portion of the agrarian population lived under the assignees. This renders the significance of the latter's role imbued with paramound importance in the Mughal administration. Most of the contemporary foreign travellers convey that the *Jagirdars* had an absolute control over the peasantry under them and governed with unbridled oppression. They lamentably noted the excessive exactions on the part of the *Jagirdar* leaving the peasantry blood white resulting usually in their plight either to the lesser oppressive territories of the native *Zamindars* (i.e. *Rajas*) or to the cities for a new vocation. Consequently, this led to the depopulation of the villages and bad tillage of the agrarian lands.[1] Some of the foreigners also observed the cruel custom of the enslavement of the cultivators and the sale of their wives and children in lieu of land revenue arrears.[2] Of all these foreign observers, Bernier in his letters to the French Finance Minster Colbert, very shrewdly analyzied the Indian agrarian problem academically. He contented that the tyrannical behaviour of the *Jagirdars* was due to two fold institutional evils. Firstly, contrary to the European practice, all lands in India were owned by the Mughal Emperor and that the *Jagirdars* unlike the French nobles, were not the proprietor landlords.[3] Secondly, the system of transfer of *Jagir* bereft the *Jagirdar* of an incentive for an investment for the improvement of the land and he mercilessly sacked the revenues regardless of the plight of the peasantry. The latter two always fearing to be fleeced never put in whole hearted toil for the cultivation of the land.[4] Thus based mostly on the testimony of the foreign observers along with his implied interpretation of Aurangzeb's well known farmers to Mohammad Hashim and Rasik Das Karori, Moreland believes in the exploitation of the peasantry by the *Jagirdars* and concludes with his theory of 'rack-renting under the whip' standing true for the entire period from Akbar to Aurangzeb.[5] Dr. Irfan Habib has simply toed the line through, of course, he has supplemented it with more evidence giving only partial analysis of the situation in hand.[6]

Apparently, it would be hard task to reject categorically the account of the foreigners unless it were contended on the basis of contemporary documentary evidence that many of their observations are based either on misunderstaing of the *Jagir* institution or too hasty generalizations which are not true of every period of the Mughal regime and are not all applicable to every territory of the vast Mughal Emprie even within the span of any single monarch's rule right from Akbar to Aurangzeb. They equally fail to take into account the geographical, ethnographic and economic factors of the various territories in Mughal India which operated against the successful working of the *Jagir* institution and rendered the remunerative position of a salaried *Jagirdar* absolutely untenable. Despite a description of the social habits and behaviour of the Indian people, they have not correlated it with the agrarian polity and its impact on the Mughal institutions. Their concept of the absolute State ownership of the land, as already discussed, was completely erroneous. They equally failed to realize that the institution of non-hereditary transferable *Tankhawh Jagir* was primarily intended to be a curb against any landed fissiparous tendency conducive to the establishment of either local despotism or semi independent 'feifs' within the Empire. The past history of India gave a sufficient note of warning that in the medieval Indian society, such an institution was indispensable for the integration and stability of a centeralised Empire.[7] It provided the Mughal Government with an obedient civil-cum-military personnel who for their career promotions lived at the mercy of the State. This class worked as counterpoise against the landed hereditary class of the *Zamindars* who could have acted as a potential danger to the stability and the existence of the Emprie. Looked both from the trends of the early 16th century and 18th century history of Northern India, it is very difficult to agree with Sir J.N. Sarkar that the institution of hereditary nobility with entrenched local landed interests like the medieval English feudal magnates would have led to the growth of a constitutional monarchy in the 16th or 17th century India.[8] Nor despite the existence of hereditary nobility did every European country evolve a constitutional monarchy. As such, a process depended on various other socio-political factors.[9] Apart from the *Zamindar* class, the Mughal nobility rested on quite different principles from the European feudal baronage and was designed to fit in the socio-political conditions of the times.[10] The review of the foreign travellers in their attempt to find deficiencies in the landed interests of the Mughal nobility as against European feudal baronage or post-feudal nobility is rather irrelevant and uncharitable. Bernier, the French scholar, had definitely a didactic approach to prove to the French Government on the basis of his observations of the Asian countries, the justification for the hereditary landed interest of the French nobility. However, he wrongly took the Mughal monarch as the absolute owner of all lands.[11] In his letters to Colbert, the platonic doctrinaire proved his contention that in all the Asian countries like Turkey, Persia and especially Hindustan, all agrarian evils flowed from the lack or right of private proprietorship on the part of the landed nobility.[12] It looks quite paradoxical that of all the European travellers, Bernier, the French physician, in order to justify the role of the 'privileged' hereditary French nobility asserted its benevolence as against the tyranny of the Mughal nobility while reserving in his mind the historic fact of the destitute condition of the pre-revolutionary French peasantry subjected to a heavy taxation of nearly 82% of its gross income.[13] It is not certain if a Mughal *Jagirdar* with hereditary rights would have shown better consideration towards his *ryots* than he did otherwise under normal peaceful circumstances. Neither his contemporary counterpart under the Dutch or the English East India Company in the small island of Bombay[14] nor his 18th century Indian successor with hereditary '*Taulakdari*' rights prove in any way more conciliatory towards his *ryots*.[15]

Any tacit recognition of the entire truthfulness of the viewpoint of the foreign travellers would reveal a great cleavage in the theory and the fact of the Mughal administration. It would mean that despite all State directives issued to the *Jagirdars* for the welfare of the *ryots* and all regulations pertaining to the assessment and collection of the revenues on the part of the assignees merely represent the paperwork of the Mughal administration and in reality were a complete farce. It equally brings out absolute failure on the part of the Mughal Government to enforce its revenue regulations promulgated from time to time on the assignees. But the contemporary documentary evidence proves the facts quite otherwise. There is no denying that at times the *Amil* of a *Jagidar* or the latter himself, if unscruplous, especially in a far distant territory did exact revenues with an oppression on the *ryots*.[16] But this cannot be taken as a general phenomenon nor did it escape the notice of the Mughal Government for taking appropriate action against the assignee. Akbar was very meticulous to enforce the Imperial revenue regulations on the assignees and the *Jagir* lands were as well administered as the *Khalsa* lands.[17] Jahangir started with great fervour to tone up the existing administration and enjoined more obligations on the part of both the *Khalsa Karori* and the *Jagirdar* for the amelioration of the *ryots*.[18] Despite his indulgence in excessive wine drinking, he showed keen sense of justice and for the major portion of his reign, the *ryots* in the *Khalsa* and the *Jagir* lands were well looked after by the administration. This is borne out by the contemporary English Records[19] and the unofficial accounts.[20] Baharistan of Mirza Nathan, even though dealing with an unsettled period of the Mughal conquest of the outyling regions and the consolidation of the Mughal rule in Bengal, Orissa, and Kuch Bihar, is a clear testimony of the spirit of Jahangir's administration. It shows that right till 1622-23 A.D., the assessment and the revenue collections, both in the *Khalsa* and the *Jagir* lands, were carried out strictly in accordance with the Imperial revenue regulations and that the provincial government of Bengal always kept a firm control over the revenue administration of the *Jagir* lands.[21] Of course, with Jahangir's failing health and ailment in the last few years of his reign, laxity of administration crept in both in the *Khalsa* and the *Jagir* lands.[22] Immediately after his accession, Shah Jahan made vigorous efforts for the improvement of the agrarian administration. The tremendous increase in the revenues within a couple of decades was not only due to the extension of the Empire but sufficiently owing to the general prosperity of the *ryots*, the extension of the agricultural land and its output both in the *Khalsa* and the *Jagir* territories.[23] According to Mohammad Sadiq, not only Shah Jahan personally but his ministers too, especially Islam Khan, Asaf Khan and above all Mohammad Sadullah Khan, took a keen interest in the agrarian uplift of all the territories and did full justice to the *ryots* in the revenue matters and considerably augmented their condition which had deteriorated in Jahangir's reign.[24] However, despite an excellent verdict on Shah Jahan's administration by the contemporary chroniclers, there is definitely an element of exaggeration in the official view point. Of course, Shah Jahan stabilized the financial position of the State[25] and benevolently cherished the good of the peasantry. [26] Whenever a glaringly oppressive act of provincial Governor or a local administrator was brought to his purview, he administered justice with sternness. But it is evident from the contemporary evidence that the local administrator and assignees exercised wider discretionary powers in their territories than their predecessors in the earlier two reigns.[28] Shah Jahan mostly left the vigilance over the details of the local revenue administration to his ministers who frequently acted on personal predictions. Though Sadullah Khan, personally capable and right, creditably (tightened) the local machinery for the betterment of the *Khalsa* administration,[29] and the brilliance of his administration was highly praised both by the contemporary and the later writers[30], his favourtism towards some of the high ranking officials and leniency even towards the incapable assignees is undeniable.[31] On Sadullah Khan's death, Mr. Jesson, an English Factor reported from Agra that during the former's administration, large sums of government dues (*Mutalba*) and loans to be recovered from the *Jagirdars* had fallen into arrears and had not been deposited in the Royal treasury. He futher comments that Shah Jahan having learnt about it after Sadullah's death revised his opinion about the deceased and did not give as much consideration to the latter's children as was usually expected.[32] So it seems that during Sadullah Khan's administration, such of the assignees who had either intimate personal contact with him or were posted in far distant places and hoped to escape Royal punishment with immunity, transgressed the Imperial regulations for the realisations of the revenues and the *ryots* of such areas definitely suffered on this account.[33] Even for the earlier phase, *Mahazar-i Shah Jahani* narrates the mal administration of some of the *Jagirdars* of a border territory of Sarkar Sehwan (*Subah* Thatta). It points out the malpractices of overassessment in some areas through the enforcement of '*Zabti*' method of assessment without proper survey and measurement, the preparation of spurious ledger accounts (*Taujih*) in which the local dignitaries (*Arabab* and *Rais*) and the *Qanungos* showed the assessment amount of their own lands against the poor *ryots*, the deviation by the local *Ijaradars* (revenue farmers) from the official schedule of rates (*Dasturul aml*) for assessment and consequently some of the *Parganas* were ruined.[34] The author of this petition regrets the absence of an *Amin* for assessment in this territory, which he comments, was otherwise a regular feature of the administration in all other parts of the Empire.[35] He openly criticizes the ineffectiveness of Shah Jahan's administration against the tyranny of some of the *Jagirdars* in Sehwan. He comments if any poor man covered all the distance to the Royal Court and brought a *farman* directed to the *Jagirdar*, the latter would not accept it and oppress the complainant out of vengeance.[36] Despite the oppression on the *ryots* and the religions grantees (*Aima*), the *Sadar, Qazi, Qanungo*, the *Zamindars* and other local dignitaries all felt helpless and were mortally afraid of the *Jagirdar*.[37] None of the *Jagirdars* would accept a *Waqai-navis* in his territory from the provincial authorites.[38] The author accuses the Central Government of the leniency shown to the negligent *Jagirdars*. While giving an instance of the oppressive administration of Ahmed Beg, he points out that on a report lodged to the provincial *Waqai-navis*, the *Jagirdars* was, of course, immediately transferred from Sehwan but instead of having been punished was promoted as the Governor of Multan.[39] The author challenges the judiciousness of the Government on this point. Such is the fearless commentary on the border administration of Shah Jahan. The author, however, concedes that the problem was singularly peculiar due to the refractory tribes of Sehwan who were responsible for unsettled conditions even in the neighbouring Sarkars of Chakar Hala and Nasirpur (*Subah* Thatta) and that the *Jagirdars* themselves accepted the assignment of these territories most reluctantly.[40]

Though the laxity of the Central Governments control over the assignees and the local administration is quite noticeable in the last phase of Shah Jahan's reign, the agrarian condition of the country suffered tremendously by the holocaust wrought by the war of succession to the Crown.[41] Aurangzeb having served as the Viceroy of Deccan along with Murshid Quli Khan, the Revenue expert as his *Diwan*, had experience of civil and revenue administration even as a Prince.[42] On his accession to the throne, imbued with a passion for serving the cause of the peasantry[43] and the betterment of the administration, he took vigorous interest in every detail of the land revenue administration. *Aurangzeb's Farman to Rasik Dass Karori* represents the real spirit with which he approached the agrarian problems for their improvement.[44] The documents of his reign reveal that the was intolerant of any derelicition on the part of the assignees and never spared any chance either for reprimanding or taking appropriate action against the defaulters.[45] Though he continued to take keen personal interest in the administration of the country to the last, he exercised a firm hold on the *Khalsa* and the *Jagir* territories right till 1681 A.D.[46] before shifting his seat of Government to Deccan. As discussed later, it is only in the second half of his reign that the agrarian administration of Northern India decayed fast.

No proper appraisal of the role of the *Jagirdar* in the Mughal administration is possible without taking into account their own difficulties and problems for the realisation of the revenues. Most of the assignees were posted at a different station than the venue of assignment. As such, they got only occasional change for personal attendance of *Jagir* management and had to leave the administration for the collection of revenues to their *Amil* and *Gumashtas* (agents). At times, the latter would indulge in excessive exactions without the least knowledge or the intention of the *Jagirdar* himself[47] though he owed full responsibility for the actions of his own revenue staff.[48] Moreover, under the rules, an assignee was obliged to afford remission to the cultivators on account of any seasonal natural calamity which always left him with an uncertain and deficient income.[49] Even an excessive bumper crop resulting in the sudden local price fall of the crops affected his income adversely.[50] All this resulted in much less income for him than his fixed emoluments. Of course, he was entitled to remission in the assessed valuation and proportionate compensation but its grant was subject to a cumbersome procedure of scrutiny and rested on the recommendation of the Central revenue ministry and the Royal discretion. Above all, the greatest problem of the *Jagirdar* was the fall in his income due to the recalcitrant attitude of some of the subjects. As a matter of Imperial policy, with the exception of petty *Jagirdars*, an assignee was allotted proportionate areas of the revenue paying (*Malguzar*) and the recalcitrant (*Zur Talb*) subjects and *Zamindars*. In comparision to the extent of the *Khalsa* territories, the over-whelming extensive portions with recalcitrant subjects, and *Zamindaries* settled on clannish basis fell to the assignees for the realisation of the revenues. This forced the *Jagirdar* and his revenue staff to resort to occasional armed action and realise the revenues through coercion and oppression. The agricultural land did not bear any appreciable sale value nor did the Mughal law permit the attachment of any immovalble property of agricultural land.[51] As the *Jagirdar's* own assignment was purely temporary, he, too, was interested only in the immediate recovery of the revenues rather than in the land. So at times, a harsh *Jagirdar* or his staff attached movable property inclusive of the ploughs and oxen of the cultivators and at places, the terrorized *royts* of their own sold wives and children in the slave market to pay the land revenue.[52] Still worse, an unscrupulous *Jagirdar* himself resorted to the inhuman practice of enslavement of the *ryots*, their wives and children and recovered his revenues from the sale proceeds of the latter from the market.[53] Akbar forbade this cruel practice[54] but it seems that it continued under his successors in such of the recalcitrant areas where the *Jagirdar* could redeem his position under the cover of the suppression of recalcitrance and the restoration of the rule of law. Though some of the foreign travellers did note that there were sections of the people and *Zamindars* in India who would nevery pay the revenues unless forced through armed action, they did not appreciate the difficulties of the assignees who were entitled to these revenues in lieu of their salaries. In their attempts at generalization, they did not make any distinction between the treatment meted out to the revenue paying (*Mal Guzar*) *ryots* and the recalcitrant (*Zur Talb*) subjects. Manrique wrote about the people of Bengal, "In spite of such violence, the Bengalese are so averse to paying money that some sections of the community hold that the payment of this tribute (land revenue) is a great humiliation, unless they have first been severly beaten. If they pay this tribute without being first well chastised, they are received very coldly by their wives, who give them in revenge, very poor meals for several days, upbraiding them with being useless men and cowards, for surrendering so easily it had cost them such pains to amass."[55] What Manrique wrote for Bengal, Manucci wrote about the whole of India. Describing that habit of evasion of the revenue payment, Manucci comments:

> "Throughout the Empire, the King is obliged to maintain *Fosdars* (*Faujdars*) that is, lords of any Army-for if had no such officers no one would pay him either revenue or tribute. For the people of India never pay without being forced....It is the peasants habit to go on refusing payment asserting that they have no money. The chastisements and the instruments are very severe........In this way, little by little, the peasants pay what they owe. This habit is much honoured amount husbandmen-that is, never to pay readily, and to undergo these torments and this disgrace is among an honour. He who gets most blows and suffers the most is the most esteemed. If per chance, the soil does not produce a crop, by reason of therein failing, they sell their sons and their cattle to meet what they are obliged to pay."[56]

Though such a general picture cannot be accepted for either the entire of Bengal or the Indian peasants as a whole, there is substantial grain of truth which can be explained only on ethnographic and geographical grounds for numerous agricultural clans in India spread over in all the provinces. For want of detailed technical knowledge of the sociological background of various parts of the country, the statements of the foreigners meant more for their own countrymen and were bound to be general. Manrique cleverly hit on the non revenue paying habit of 'some sections of the community' of Bengal and Manucci wrote at the fag end of Auranzeb's reign when the recalcitrance was widespread and the agrarian situation was sufficiently blurred. But it cannot be denied that all through the Mughal age, depending on the geographical situation and traditional clannish habits of the people, there were recalcitrant (*Zur Talb*) tribal settlements practically in every province. But they were more pronouneed in the outlying *Parganas* of Sehwan and Bhakkar (*Subahs* of Thatta and Multan)[57] the *Rehgar, Dogars* and *Gujars* settlements in the *Parganas* of and around Lakhi Jungle (*Subah* Delhi)[58] and Mewat, settlements in Mewat (*Subah* Ajmer)[59], some of the notoriously recalcitrant tribes in *Subah* Agra[60], especially the *Jat* settlements around Mathura and Agra[61], the sub-mountaneous regions of the *Subahs* of Malwa and Gujrat and the border territories of Bengal and Orissa, Kuch Bihar and Assam (*Subah* Bengal)[62]. Though the contemporary Persian chronicles and the official records simply characterize such named tribes as rioteous

(*Musfasid*) and recalcitrant (*Zur Talb*)[63] without giving any insight into their sociological traits, *Mahazar-i Shah Jahani* gives a detailed enthnographic description of the various groups of peoples divided into various tribes with further subdivisions settled in the territories of *Subah* Thatta and in the *Sarkars* of Bhakkar and Sehwan (*Subah* Singh).[64] It divides the tribes into two main classes, settled cultivators and non-cultivators. The cultivators class is further divided into revenue paying (*Raiyati* and *Malguzar*) and recalcitrant (*Mutmarid* and *Sarkash*). The latter would never pay anything in land revenue, except through armed coercion and always required large forces to be maintained in their territories for the realisation of the revenues and the maintenance of law and order. Unless reduced to submission as peaceful cultivators, they would render the income of *Pargana* assigned in *Tankhwah Jagir* to practical nullity.[65] Though some of the tribes always remained recalcitrant[66], others were reduced to peaceful revenue paying cultivators.[67] Similarly, for Shah Jahan's reign, the letters of Nawab Muzaffar Khan, the *Faujdar* and *Diwan* of *Chakla* Hissar, Jalal Hissari and Balkrishan deal with the recalcitrant tribes in the *Parganas* of Thata, Bhatinda, Kaithal, and Thanaser in Lakhi Jungle, *Sarkar* Sarhind (*Subah* Delhi)[68] and also the refractory tribes in *Chakla* Gwaliar (*Subah* Agra).[69] Many such recalcitrant agrarian tribes were armed and would fight not only in self defence for the evasion of the land revenue but finding an appropriate opportunity or any weakness on the part of the authorities would assume an aggressive role and resort to plunder and pillage of the revenue paying *ryots* and the poor subjects of the neighbouring territories.[70] The atomized socio-political order based on tribalism or casteism and strategically protected by the large spread jungles, ravines and hilly tracts in various regions of northern India always acted as stimulus for the refractory habits of the recalcitrant clans in defiance of the established rule of law.[71] The Mughal Government, on the other hand, was sufficiently handicapped by the primitive means of communication and transport as well as the natural obstacles caused by the geographical features of specific regions.[72] By the time a punitive expedition was launched, a considerable harm to the crops and the properties of the revenue paying subjects of the surrounding vaillages was already done.[73] Despite the strong, centralized and stable Mughal Empire, it must be conceded that a conflict between the Government collectors or assignees and such recalcitrant tribes was a constant phenomenon in one or another region throughout the Mughal age. Of course, after successful, military operations, a deterrent punishment was inflicted with a view to either the entire extermination of the habitually recalcitrant clan or its reduction to peaceful revenue paying riaya after heavy toll of life.[74]

Thus with an assignment in a recalcitrant area, the fall in the revenues of a *Jagirdar* as against the assessed valuation remained a constantly troublesome feature throughout the Mughal age.[75] Though the Government was committed to afford remission in the valuation of assignment and proportionate compensation[76], it is rather doubtful that all assignees were always compensated on this account. A *Jagirdar* was naturally constrained to exert his utmost authority for the realisation of the revenues through military action, at times even backed by the local *Faujdar*.[78] With grater resources at command, this inevitably led to tyranny and oppression on the part of the Mughal officials.[79] Usually, the recalcitrant settlements were reduced to submission for the payment of the land revenue[80] but if they persisted in obstinacy, they would be completely rooted out of their territories and replaced by revenue paying tribes and subjects.[81] Though the process of forcing the recalcitrant settlements in Northern India to submission and bringing them around to the civilising character of revenue payment continued on an extensive scale right through middle of Aurangzeb's reign[82], thereafter the situation with a reverse gear drifted towards catastrophe. So far, the *Jagir* system had stood the occasional disturbance on the part of the earmarked recalcitrant territories and had worked quite satisfactorily for the purposes designed. Though it had already suffered a first round in Auranzeb's reign because of the disturbed agrarian conditions wrought by the Marhattas in the Deccan and Gujrat,[83] the shifting of the Mughal Court to Deccan in 1681 A.D., the constant warfare against the Deccanite Muslim states and Marhattas and above all the widespread unrest in various portions of Northern India shook the complicated machinery of the *Jagir* system to its very foundations. All this gave a further edge to the recalcitrance of the various clans and *Zamindars* for the evasion of the land revenue payment practically in all the provinces of Northern India. Izad Baksh, the author of *Riyazul-Vidad*, writing in 1686 A.D., noted with regret the lack of proper control of the Central Governemnt, the growing spirit of lawlessness around Agra, Delhi and other places, the refractory attitude of the *Zamindars* and the consequent fall in the income of the *Jagirs*. The author underlines a marked contrast between the rule of law in the earlier phase of Aurangzeb's reign and the growing uncertainty of the day.[84] The political situation acquired a still more serious turn by the close of the 17th century and the opening years of the 18th century before Aurangzeb' death in 1707 A.D.[85] As a recalcitrant local Zamindar claimed beter loyalty from his clansmen for the realisation of the revenues, the conflict between an assignee and the *Zamindar* was fast becoming a general feature of the north Indian agrarian life.[86] Moreover, in such an uncertain atmosphere, it became difficult for an ordinary *Jagirdar* to profect the revenues of his *Jagir* from forcible and illegal realisation either by the *Amil* of a neighbouring *Jagir*[87] or a neighbouring *Karori*[88] and his territory was not immune from the imposition of the illegal *Faujdari* dues.[89] Thus an assignee's problem of the fall in income as against his fixed emoluments became very severe and rendered his economic position absolutely untenable. At places, he could not meet even the expenses of the contigent meant for the very realisation of the revenues nor could he stand the expenditure of the rations of the stables maintained.[90] Sometimes, he could not realise even half of the revenues and still at other places practically nothing.[91] He made repeated petitions for either the transfer of the *Jagir* to a trouble free area or reinforcement from the *Faujdar* for the recovery of the revenues from the recalcitrants.[92] The assignment of a *Jagir* lost its original charm and was no longer coveted by an ordinary *Mansabdar* as against a cash salary. Apart from the *Tankhwah Jagir*, a *Mansabdar* entrusted with the suppression of the recalcitrants usually expected an *Inam Jagir* unconditional of the maintenance of any additional Army.[93]

The shortage in income due to the evasion of payment of land revenue by the recalcitrant *ryots* or *Zamindars* landed many a *Mansabdars* in financial embarrassment. As they had to maintain troop contingents and full establishment for the administration of the *Jagirs*, they often ran into debts. They had to borrow money on interest either from the State or private money lenders (*Sarafs*). This problem, already quite actue in certain portions of the reign of Shah Jahan,[94] acquired an extremely serious turn in Aurangzeb's reign.[95] Consequently, for getting ready cash money in hand, many a *Jagirdar* passed on their assignments to the revenue farmers (*Mustajirs*) on much less value of the *Jagir* than on the customary rates as collection charges. At times, the agents of the revenue farmers tried to extort maximum realisations and indiscriminately acted callously towards the *Raiyti* (revenue paying) and recalcitrant subjects.

Though himself a victim of the imbecility of the Mughal Government, at places an assignee or his *Amil* did not hesitate to exploit the growing prospects of the times and hardpressed both the local *Zamindars* and the *ryots* with over realisation of the revenues.[96] All the same, in the major portions of northern India, the Mughal Government through its directives claimed better official control on the illegitimate activities of the assignees than on the ever increasing recalcitrance on the part of the local *Zamindars* and the *ryots*.

On the other hand, contradictory as it apparently seems, the non-availability of the reserved *Jagir* (*Paibaqi*) lands for further assignment fast became a marked feature in the second half of Aurangzeb's reign[98] though the situation in Northern India was not as acute as in the Deccan. The original archives of Aurangzeb's reign clearly point towards the abundant availability of the *Paibaqi* lands till 1680 A.D.[99] But thereafter the situation gradually drifted into a crisis. The Deccan had already been deficit in the *Paibaqi* lands. In Shah Jahan's reign, most of the *Mansabdars* serving in Deccan also wanted *Jagirs* over there but the Deccan revenues could not stand this pressure and invariably many an assignment had to be made in the North[100] or in parts at both the places.[101] In Aurangzeb's reign, despite the conquest of Bijapur (1686 AD) and Golkanda (1687 A.D.), the position of *Paibaqi* lands in the Deccan remained very tight[102] and the pressure of assignments in the North became stronger. Such a phenomenon was inevitable in the wake of the vast expansion of the Mughal bureaucracy,[103] the military establishment needed for the conquest and thereafter the administration of the Deccanite states,[104] the political expediency for the absorption of many of the erstwhile Deccani State servants as *Mansabdars*[105] and the fresh appointments of local *Zamindars* alongwith assignment of *Jagirs* and *Mansabs*.[106] To this was added the most distrurbing factor of the drastic fall in the income of the assignments caused by the Marhatta depredations in the Mughal territories and the realisation of the revenues in connivance with the local *Zamindars* and some of the tenants.[107] Bhim Sen notes that many of the Mughal *Parganas* had been regularly assigned by the Marhattas amongst themselves and the Mughal *Mansabdars* did not possess even adequate contingents for the realisation of the revenues. Thus with double set of parallel *defacto* and *dejure Jagirdars*, the Marhattas and the Mughals, whenever the *Amils* of the latter approached the *ryots* for the revenues, they had nothing to realise excepting squeezing the blood of the peasantry.[108] The *Jagirdars* constantly beseeched the Mughal Government for the assignments in the North or in any other *Paibaqi* land which became a mirage in Deccan.[109] The *Jagir* situation in the North, though better than in the Deccan, was also fast approaching a crisis in the disturbed territories but the climax of the *Jagir* crises came after Aurangzeb's death.[110] All the same, it cannot be denied that during the last two decades of Aurangzeb's reign, the institution of *Jagir* gave way to the unsettled socio-political conditions of the country and registered a first chapter in the process of its own complete breakdown and the disintegration of the Mughal Empire.

Footnotes

1. Pelsaert's Remonstrantie, '*Jahangir's India*', tr. by Moreland & Geyl, Cambridge, 1925, p. 47; Manrique. *F.S. Travels*, 1629-43, tr. Luard, *Hakluyt Society* (2 vols), London, 1907-08 vol. I. pp. 52-53; Vol II p. 272. De Laet, *The Empire of the Great Mogal.*, tr. by Hoyland and Banerjee, pp. 94-95; *Traverniers' Travels in India*, ed. V. Ball, Vol. I p. 391; Bernier Francois, pp. 224-25; Manucci Niccolao, '*Storia Do Mogor*', tr. by William Irvine, Vol. II, pp. 451-52. (St. Xavier, tr. Hosten, J.A.S.B., N.S. XXIII, 1927. IInd letter dated 14th Sept. 1609, p. 121).

2. Manrique, I. p. 53; Pelsaert, p. 47; Bernier, p. 205.

3. Bernier, p. 226 comments, "From what I have said a question will naturally arise, whether it would not be more advantageous for the king as well as for the people if the former ceased to be sole possessor of the land, and the right of private property were recognised in the Indies as it is with us? I have carefully compared the condition of the European states, where that right is acknowledged, with the condition of those countries where it is not known, and am persuaded that the absence of it among the people is injurious to the best interests of the sovereign himself".

4. *Ibid.* Bernier puts the problem thus : "...The peasant cannot avoid asking himself this question. Why should I toil for a tyrant who may come tomorrow and lay his rapacious hands upon all I possess and value, without leaving me, if such should be his humour, the means to drag on my miserable existence? The *Timariots*, Governors, and Revenue Contractors, on their own part reason in this manner : 'Why should the neglected State of this land create uneasiness in our minds? And why should we expend our own money and time to render it fruitful? We may be deprived of it in a single moment, and our exertions would benefit neither ourselves nor our children. Let us draw from the soil all the money we can, though the peasant should starve or abscond, and we should leave it, when commanded to quit, a dreary wilderness."

5. Moreland, '*Agrarian system*' pp. 129-138, 142-149; and '*From Akbar to Aurangzeb*', p. 203; *Address to the Indian Section of the Royal Society of Arts*, London, A summary of the paper vide Civil and Military Gazette of Lahore, dated Ist April 1929.

6. Irfan M.Habib vide article, 'The Agrarian Causes of the Mughal Empire' in '*Enquiry* no. 2, pp. 82-92; '*Enquiry*' No. 3, pp. 74-76.

7. '*A Report on the Land Tenures and Special Powers of Certain Thikanedars of the Jaipur State*' by C.U. Wills, pp. 8-10. Wills, in his brilliant analysis of the impact of the Mughal Jagir system on the princely family of Amber emphasizes the importance of the institution of transferable *Jagir* during the Mughal age. He has rightly criticized Moreland for following the viewpoint of the foreign travellers. He comments, "The peculiarity in the system is that though an employee's sanctioned salary might remain unchanged, it was improbably that he would retain the same area as Jagir,

in lieu of that salary for any length of time. When he was transferred from one post to another, his *Jagir* would be changed, and even without such a transfer, the assignment would frequently be shifted.... Moreland emphasizes the agrarian instability which resulted from these constant changes; but to create the insecurity in the tenure of the State's employees seems to have been the settled policy of the Mughal Emperors. The effect of this system of short, shifting assignments upon the position of the Kachhwaha chiefs of Amber can be easily understood. Their family had, ever since the time of Raja Bihari Mal, been holding high positions under the Moughal Emperors, for which like any one else, they were remunerated by assignments; but these *Jagirs* had no permanence, except in that portion which formed their patrimony of *Watan*. Normally, the *Watan* was constant, whereas the Raja's ordinary assignments were continuously shifted with the deliberate purpose of preventing him from stabilising his territorial interest. While, therefore, the hereditary estates which the Amber house enjoyed by no means represented the whole of the territory under their control, yet it was the only permanent nucleus upon which they could depend. Tod's account of the position at the end of the 17th century emphasises this territorial weakness." Though Wills has examined the position with regard to the hereditary *Zamindars* (Rajas) who held *Mansabs*, the same analysis is equally applicable to the big *Mansabdars* who held only *Tankhawh Jagirs*. On account of the enforcement of military and financial regulations, a few instances of revolt on the latter's part can be quoted. (For revolt in Bihar and Bengal in the 23rd R.Y. of Akbar, See A.N.II tr. Bev. pp. 418-29; Mirza Yusuf Khan, the Governor of Kashmir's revolt in the 36th R.Y. of Akbar vide *Ain*. I. Blochmann. pp. 370-71; Mahabat Khan's revolt in Jahangir's reign. The situation would have been far worse with landed hereditary *Mansabdars* and this would have another serious factor for the political instability throughout the Mughal age.

8. Sarkar, *Mughal Adminstration*, pp. 155-57.

9. Despite the existence of a feudal state of society, France did not have any constitutional monarchy before the work of the National Assembly after the French Revolution (1789), Piedmont (Italy), before the 19th Centruy and Germany failed to evolve any constitutional monarchy whatsoever.

10. The rough analogy of the fact that the Mughal nobility owed military service to the State and that the *Tankhawh Jagirdars* lived by the appropriation of social surplus produced by the peasantry did not render it by any means as a feudal class in the European concept. It did not acquire any traits of 'fief' holding knighthood and the feudal rights and obligations as prevelant in medieval Europe. The *Zamindars* (*Rajas* and *Rais* etc.) holding *Mansabs* alongwith hereditary *Watan-Jagir* (Partimony) were, however, nearer to the European feudal concept though their additional salary *Jagirs* were subject to the same regulations and applicable to the non-hereditary Mughal nobility. Of course, Bernier (Vide pp. 226, 230) regretted the existence of a non-hereditary nobility in most of the Asian countires, Turkey, Persian

and India and also in Egypt (Africa) but he failed to realise the socio-political background of the Eastern civilisations. In medieval feudal England or France, the monarchy was regarded as an apex of feudal civilisation while the real power was diffused into the hands of multitude of feudal magnates. With the emergence of a centerlised nation state in the 16th century, though the political power of feudal baronage was suppressed, its hereditary landed interests were retained. But in an Asian country, especially India, any delegation of political and military power to hereditary landed magnates would have resulted not only in a week monarchy but also as an inevitable course of parcelling out the state into various independent principalities. Dr. Tara Chand, *Freedom Movement in India* I, Introduction, pp. 9-38; Wittogel, *Oriental Despotism,* pp. 81-85.

11. In this respect, Bernier was deceived by the institution of *Jagir* transfer and could not distinguish between the Indian concept of land ownership from other countries like Eygpt, Turkey and Persia.

12. Bernier, vide p. 230 comments, "those three countries, Turkey, Persia, and Hindoustan...having lost that respect for the right of property, which is the basis of all that is good and useful in the world, necessary resemble each other in essential points, they fall into the same pernicious errors, and must, sooner or later, experience the natural consequences of those errors-tyranny, ruin, and misery...How happy and thankful should we feel, My Lord, that in our quarter of the Glooe, kings are not the sole proprietors of the soil! Were they so, we should seek in vain for countries well cultivated and populous, for well built and opulent cities, for a polite, contented, and flourishing people."

13. *Ibid.*

14. *The English Factories* 1665-67, pp. 72-73; 288; 1668-69, pp. 216-17, 223.

15. Moreland, '*Agrarian System*', pp. 172-179. Dr. Tara Chand, '*Freedom Movement in India*, I. pp. 170-71.

16. In Akbar's reign, after the conquest of Sindh, Saiyyad Mohammad Mir Adal, the *Jagirdar* of Bhakkar enforced the method of *Kankut* assessment in *Pargana* Kakri against the notions of just assessment' (5 *maunds* per *bigha*) and came in armed conflict with the Mangaicha tribe of the *Pargana* forcing the latter tribe to fight. Saiyyad Abul Fazl, son of Mir Adal, the next assignee imprisoned the *Muqaddams* and even got trampled two of them under the elephant's feet. (vide *Tarkih-i-Singh*, printed Pers. Text pp. 245-46; *Mahzar-i-Shahjahani*, Pp. 9-10). Also A.N. Br. M. Add. 26, 207, fol. 228b; *Mahzar-i-Shahjahani*, pp. 107, 145-47, 154-63.

17. A.N. Br. M.Add. or. 27, 247, fols 331b-33b; Ms. Add. 26, 207, fols 160a-162b. The 27th year reforms of Todar Mal specifically mention the obligations on the part of the *Amils* of the *Jagirdars*. For the prompt action taken against the *Gumashta* and the *Shiqdar* for oppression on the *ryots* in Kashmir, see details A.N. Add. 26, 207, 34th R.Y.Fol 228b; for the

enforcement of revenue reforms in Kashmir, *Ibid.* 42 R.Y. fol 303a; for the enforcement of the general orders in both the *Khalsa* and the *Jagir* lands, *Ibid*, 25th R.Y. fol 147a, 39th R.Y. fol 275b., *Mahzari Shahjahan*, pp. 63-65 while tracing the past history of the *Jagirdars* in *Thatta* and *Sehwan* the outlying portion of the Mughal Empire, excepting the untoward incident of enforcing the *Kankut* system by highly praising the administration of the *Jagirdars* under Akbar.

18. *Tuzuk-i-Jahangiri* M.S Rampur, p. 9-11, tr. Rogers, pp. 7-10. Apart from the abolition of the cesses of *Tamgha*, river tolls and other cesses which the *Jagirdars* had pocketed so far, the latter were enjoined to build *Sarais* (inns), mosques, and dig wells for the growth and prosperity of the population and also to build hospitals at the State expenditure in the big cities under their terriroties. *Akbar Nama* Br. M.Add. 26, 207 fol 275b also records a general directive issued to the *Jagirdars* in the 39th R.Y. for looking after the prosperity of the *ryots* but Jahangir is more explicit in his memoirs. Also see *Jahangir Namah*, Ms. Aligarh, fols 14a-14b; *Maasir-i-Jahangiri*, Ms. 563 Patna, fols 331-34b.

19. *The English Factory Records* give full credit to Jahangir's administration for the compliance of the Royal orders, the rule of law and the full co-operation they received from the local administration. See *The English Factories in India* (1622-23), pp. 250-51.

20. *Waqai Asad Beg*, Ms. Aligarh, pp. 138-39. *Inshai Abdul Latif*, Ms. R.A.S.B. Calcutta, fols 2a-3b.

21. *Baharistan*, Ms. Paris, fols 61b, 285a-286a; 311b.

22. *Amil Salih* Pr. Text I. p. 319; P.N. Warris, pp. 12-13. The other historians of Shah Jahan's reign (vide Qazvini, p. 452; Mulakhas, fols 348a-b; Mohd. Sadiq, p.14) have scandalously dubbed Jahangir's character given to sloth and pleasure and with a self-interest for the elevation of Shah Jahan's reign have characterized the entire administration of Jahangir as a failure. In this respect, the later historians showed better consideration to Jahangir and noted laxity of administration only in the last years of his reign. Rai Bindra Ban in *Lubul Tawarikh* written in Aurangzeb's reign (Ms. 954/15f, S.A.S. Aligarh, fols 81a-82a) comments that Akbar's revenue regulations were continued throughout Jahangir's administration. Though Jahangir administered justice with complete impartiality and sternness, the last years of his reign were marked by the deterioration in the standard of honesty and integrity on the part of the revenue officials of the *Parganas*. Also see *Tofatul Hind* by Lal Ram, Ms. Br. M.Rieu I, 236a, Add. 658, fols 396b-398b).

23. Lahori Pr. Text II. pp. 709-13; Mohd. Sadiq, p.14, Mulakhas, fols 346b-348b.

24. Mohd. Sadiq, p. 14.

25. Qazwini (Ms. Rampur, p. 452) states that having inherited a depleted treasury, Shah Jahan ordered in the very 3rd R.Y. after accession, that 7 *karor dams* should be reserved for the *Khalsa* and that the state expenditure was fixed at I *kror* Rupees a year which could rise upto 1 *kror* and 20 *lacs* only ihn abnormal circumstances.

26. *Shah Jahan's Farman* dated 5th R.Y. issued to Zafar Khan, the Governor of Kashmir (vide *Qazwini*, Ms. Br. M.I 258b (or 173) pp. 509-10; *Amal-i-Salih*, Printed text. I, pp. 543-46) abolishing certain local oppressive cesses. For the information of the subjects, the *Farman* was inscribed on a marble stone on the gate of the Grand-Mosque (Jama Masjid) Srinagar; also administrative reforms in the 6th R.Y. in *Subah* Lahore vide *Amal-i Salih*, Pr. Text II, pp. 7-8.

27. *Ibid*. Removal of Itiqad Kha, the *Subahdar* of Kashmir and appointment of Zafar Khan also for the confiscation of the property and imprisonment of Nasir Khan, the Governor of Gujrat, see Bentley Richard, *The Political and Statistical History of Gujrat*, London, 1835 (based on Mohammed Ali khan's *Mirat-i-Ahmadi*, tr. James Bird) p.378.

28. *The English Factories* (1651-54, pp. 49-50) Richard Davidge, *The English Factor at Agra* (vide his letter dated March 8, 1651 A.D. p. 50) for his commercial transaction, did not accept a general order from Sadu Ilah Khan, the minister directed to the Governor of Surat thinking that it would not be obeyed, "it being only that the Governor of Surat should in all points obey the Firmand." and wanted specific orders in the names of the officials concerned. For assignees, see *Mahzar-i-Shah Jahani*, pp.114a-114b.

29. *Kh. Siyaq*, Ms. Aligarh, 16a, Ms. N.A.I. p. 32; Khwafi Khan I, pp. 759-60.

30. Aurangzeb was a great admirer of Sadda Ullah Khan and in his letters highly praises his ability, integrity and industry. See *Raqiam Kariam*, Ms. Rampur, p. 46, 58. Of the later writers, see *Munshiat Anand Ram* Ms. 865 Patna, fols 74a-74b; *Lubul Tawarikh- i Hind* of Bindra Ban, fols 83b-84b; Khwafi, I pp. 731-36; M.I. Br. M. fol 51a-52b.

31. *The English Factories* (1655-60), p. 62. report that Hafif Mahmud alias Shaikh Mahmud Amin proved dishonest (covetuous) as *Diwan* of Agra and was transferred as *Amin* of Sambhar (*Subah* Ajmer). As he was a favourite of Sadda Ullah Khan, he was later appointed as the Governor of Surat.

32. *Ibid*., pp. 66-67.

33. *Ibid*. (1646-50), p. 127. The factory records condemn the administration of Shaista Khan, the Governor of Gujrat. The editor of *The English Factories* (1655-60) pp. 1-2, in his introduction condemns the administration of Sadaullah Khan. He comments, "...All the writers of the time extol the splendour of his court, the liberality of his rule, and his personal popularity. All the same, they do not conceal the fact this splendid façade hid a crumbling interior. Such extravagant expenditure was a crushing burden upon the

resources of the country, while the vinality of the officials, and the tyrannical caprice of the local Governors, added to the misery of the people who had little or no means of obtaining redress"...;Also *Mahazar-i-Shahjahani*, pp. 45-48.

34. *Mahzar-i Shah Jahani*, pp. 18-22, 51-53

35. *Ibid.* The petition to Shah Jahan recommends that an official *Amin* should be appointed in the Sehwan territory who would enforce the assessment on the *Jagirdars* on the basis of the official *Dasturulaml*. (Schedule of rates) and that in every *Pargana*, the *Shiqdar* and the *Karkun* should of their own distribute the assessment on the *ryots* and finally the *Shiqdar* should not be allowed to function only as the *Jagirdar's* official for the purposes of assessment.

36. *Ibid.* p. 174.

37. *Ibid.*

38. *Ibid.* pp. 175-77. In the tenure of Dinar Kha (who was the *Jagirdar* when the petition was submitted in 1044 A.H., a *Waqainavis* named Niamat Ullah was executed by the insurgents right below the gate of the fort and no notice about it was taken by the higher authorities. A *Waqainavis*, a representative of Man Singh, the *Waqainavis* of Bhakkar left after a short period. For the third time, the *Bakshi* of Thatta sent his own *Gumashta* (representative) as *Waqainavis* but even he was not accepted by Dinar Khan, the *Jagirdar*.

39 *Ibid.* p. 177.

40. *Ibid.* p. 180.

41. Sarkar, Aurangzeb vol V, pp. 80-81.

42. Adab, pp. 55-57, 64-68, 71-72, 75-77, 87-88, 199-200, 227-228, 279-80, 231-33. Aurangzeb's letters to Shahjahan and his ministers reveal his full grasp over the technical details of the land revenue administration of Deccan and his sterling qualities as an administrator working for the good of the *ryots*. Also see Sarkar, '*Aurgangzeb*' vol. V, pp. 116-17.

43. *Ibid.*, p. 87-88; *Aurangzeb's Letter to Prince Azam*, Sarkar's Aurangzeb, Vol . p 259; also Raqiam Kariam, pp. 109-110.

44. R.D. Ms. Or. Oct., 113 J, Berlin fol Ib-8b; *Nigar Nama* Ms. Bod. Oxfd. fols 127a-128b.

45 See '*Checks on the Jagirdar*', footnote 7.

46. R.A.J. *Akhbarat*, Reg No. 361 dated 23rd of *Hurah*, 25th R.Y., 1092 A.H. 24th November 1681 A.D. Rashid Khan, *Diwan-i Khalsa* issued an order for enquirty into the administration of the *Khalsa* and the *Jagirlands* and for a report on the disturbed '*Ghair amli*' *Mahals*.

47. *Ain* tr. Blochmann. I., p. 328; *Tarikh-i-Mahsumi* Pr. Text. p. 247 mentioned the benevolent treatment of Masand-i-Ali Fateh Khan, the *Jagirdar* of

Bhakkar (*Subah* Sindh) but in his absence, his *Vakil* (Agent) named Shahbaz Khan oppressed the *ryots* and was killed in an armed conflict; also *Maktubat-i Khan Jahan*, fols 63a-654b; *Mahazar-i Shah Jahani*, pp. 154-63; *Waqai Ranthanbore*, p. 386.

48. *Ibid.* Most of the *Jagirdars* were transferred on such a complaint against them. *Mahzar-i Shah Jahani* states that Ahmed Beg Khan, the *Jagirdar* of Sehwan was very considerate towards his *ryots* but he left the administration in the hands of his brothers Mirza Yusuf who committed atrocities on the *ryots*. The Author holds the *Jagirdar* responsible for it and does not think that the simple punishment of transfer of the assignee was adequate.

49. See different *Takhfif* documents quoted early in the portion dealing with '*Jagir* System'.

50. *Ibid.*

51. M.H.*Mirat* I., pp. 269-172.

52. *Maktubat-i-Khan Jahan*, Br. M. fol 63a. In some areas, a few tribes of their own, when forced, paid the land revenue in terms of cattle and animals. *Mahzar-i Shah Jahani* p. 85 quotes the practice of *Sanriya*, a recalcitrant tribe in *Sarkar* Sehwan paying the land revenue only when forced by the *Jagirdar* and make the payment not in cash or kind (crop share) but in terms of camels, cows and asses. *Mahzar-i Shahjahani* pp. 21-22; (in *Sarkar* Bhakkar, *Subah* Multan); *Murraqat-i Hashim*, the *Diwan* of Orissa for appression on *ryots*). Badauni, (Ms. *Elliot* Bod. Oxford, fols 257b-258a) narrates this evil practice in Akbar's reign even in the *Khalsa* territories after the 19th R.Y. *Karori* experiment. Manucci (II. p. 451) blames the people for this selfish and cruel custom.

53. Pelsaert, '*Jahangir's India*' tr. Moreland, p. 47; Manrique I, p. 53 comments for Bengal that only heathens, i.e non-Muslims were enslaved and auctioned; Also II, p. 272; Bernier, p. 205. This cruel practice of the sale of debtors continued in India till early 19th century when it was abolished by the British Government. Hamilton (East India, I.P. 121) notes that he himself was empowered to sell up the families of his creditors in *Tatta* without going to the Court. Also see J.Talboys Wheeler, *History of India*, 1881, Vol. II, part II, p. 423.

54. *A.N.* Tr. Bev. II. pp. 159-60.

55. Manbrique, I., pp. 53-54.

56. Manucci, 450-51.

57. *Mahazar-i Shah Jahani*, pp. 75-77.

58. *Maktubat-i Khan Jahan*, Br. M.fols 48a, 62b, 52a-52b, 55b-56b; *Khulastu-i Tawarikh* of Sujjan Rai Ms. Br. M; fols 53b-54a; Manucci; II, pp. 457-58.

59. Pelsaert, *Jahangir's India*, p. 15; Manucci, II, p. 459; *Amal-i Sabih*, Pr. Text, III, pp. 110-12.

60. A.N. Pers. Text. II, p.163; III, p. 231; *Tuzuki-i Jahangiri* tr. Rodgers, pp. 98-99; Lahori I, pp. ii, 71-72, 76; II, p. 425; *The English Factories* (1665-60), pp. 65-67.

61. R.A.J. *Vakil Reports*, No. 369-239 dated 28th *Shaban* 34th R.Y. 1101 AH/ 17th May, 1690 A.D; also 596-1319 30th R.Y. also category no. 4 reg 149 (Aurangzeb's reign) Isar Das, fol 53a; Manucci, II, pp. 223-4; *Ma'asir-i Alamgiri*, p. 93; *Riyaz-al Wudad*, Br. M, fols 16b, 18a-18b.

62. For Orissa, *Muraqqat-i Hasan*, fols 252-56; for Kuch Bihar, Mamuri Ms. Rampur, pp. 449-50; Fatehi Ibriya, Ms. Orient, 266 fol 55a-55b; *Mufid ul Insha*, fols 48b-49a, 71a-74a; For Bengal, Gujrat and Malwa, op. cit., footnotes 17 & 18 of *the Impact of the Zamindari System*.

63. *Ibid.* op. cit., 57, 58, 59.

64. *Mahzar-i Shahjahani*, pp. 82-87. The author divides the people into *Grohs*, every *Groh* into *Kaom* (Tribe), every *Kaom* into *Firqas* (Sub-tribes) and every *Firqa* into *Jamahi* (tribe unit).

65. *Ibid.* p. 36. For example, the tribes of Sahuda, Sameja-kibrya and Sameja Dal completely desolated the *Pargana* Samwati (*Sarkar* Nasr Pur, *Subah* Thatta) which was otherwise worth 40 *lacs* of salary *dams*. Similary, the insurgent tribes of *Pargana* Halkandi (which was worth the revenue of II thousand *Kharwar* ass loads) of corn in the tenure of Muzaffar Khan's Governorship (Jahangir's reign) completely ruined it. They even executed Haji Mohammad, the *Shiqdar*. (*Ibid.* pp. 36-38).

66. *Ibid.* The author himself catagorises in detail the turbulent tribes (pp. 83-85) and comments that some of the groups from the tribes of Samajehs, Mangiwanas and Unnas had always been rebellious and never paid land revenue without coercion. Similarly, the tribes of Sahuda, Sameja Kibrya and Sameja Dal in *Pargana* Samwati (*Sarkar* Nasrpur *Subah* Thatta), the tribes of Dal and Shora in the sub-mountaineous region of *Sarkar* Chakar Hala (pp. 45-48), the Baloch tribes of Tayabeh, in *Pargana* Bhagban (*Sarkar* Sehwan p. 63), Juneja tribe in *Pargana* San with four sub-divisions (pp. 75-77), Samejahs in a Tappa of *Pargana* Lakut (pp. 79-80) were always recalcitrant and never paid land revenue without armed conflict. Also see '*The Journal of Sir Thomas Roe*' (vide his description of the extent of the Mughal Empire) which notes the Balochs of Bhakkar as "a kind of rude war like people". Also Shah Jahan's original *Farman* (R.A.J. No. 76/139 dated 12th of *Rajab* 1060 A.H. 24th R.Y. addressed to Mirza Raja Jai Singh for the suppression of the insurgents in Sehwan; also *The English Factories* (1665-60) vide a letter dated 21st Feb, 1656 p. 77,.narrating the rebellion of Baluchs in Sindh.

67. *Ibid.*, pp. 11-13. For example, the tribe of Samajeh with two branches Rajyal and Bhan in *Pargana* Bela (*Sarkar* Bhakkar) were recalcitrant till the 15th R.Y. of Jahangir's reign but after reduction became revenue paying (*Raiyti*) cultivators, The area also prospered. Similarly, Muzaffar Khan Mahmuri,

the Governor of Thatta suppressed the well-known recalcitrant tribes of Dal, Daud Shora and Shora, He reducted the insurgent tribe of Daud Shora into *Raiyti* which did not show any recalcitrance thereafter. (pp. 48-53).

68. *Maktubat-i Khan Jahan*, Br. M. fols 48a, 62b, 52a-52b, 55b-56b, 115a.

69. *Ibid.*, fols 2a-2b, 4a, 7a. The tribes of Patwar, Bhakkarwali Malhai and Attatri are mentioned as recalcitrant.

70. *Maktubati-i Khan Jahan*, Br. M.Fols 7a-7b makes such statement for the tribes of Chakla Gwalior (*Subah* Agra); *Mahzar-i Shah*, pp. 6-8, 10-11, 36-38, 82-88. *The English Factories* 1655-60, pp. 65-66; *Akbar Nama* gives a general description for such phenomenon vide f.no. 69; *Ain*, Jarrett. II. p. 207 make a general statement regarding the people of Malwa, "The peasants and even grain dealers are never without arms."

71. *Ibid.* Jahangir (vide *Tuzuk*, p. 125 tr. Rodgers) comments on the habitual recalcitrant behaviour of the '*Ganwars* (rustics) and cultivators' on the eastern side of Jamuna near Mathura." For detail of tribal and caste structure, op. cit., Dr. Tara Chand, (*History of the Freedom Movement*', I, pp. 87-88) very aptly comments, " What India lacked however, was the conscisouness of oneness-social and political unity. Even in periods when one political system dominated the whole country, the sense of fellowship in a social community or of willing obedience to a common authority was lacking. Neither cultural homogeneity nor political overlordship succeeded in breaking down the barriers which divided groups, societies and people of India."

72. Despite the construction of roads and highways by Sher Shah and Akbar, the problem of communication in the vast interior countryside remained constant until the building of network of railway and roads in the 19th and 20th centuries under the British rule in India. Also see Dr. Tara Chand, '*History of Freedom Movement*', I, pp. 77-78.

73. *A.N.* Ms. Br. M.Add 27, 247 fol 332; *Mahzar-i Shah Jahani*, pp. 36-38; *The English Factories* (1655-60), pp. 65-67, records the insurrection of the "*Gomors*' (*Gunwars* i.e. rustics and not *Gaonwar,* i.e. villagers as edited) on the death of Sadullah Khan in several of his *Jagir* 'Towns near Agra' and the plunder of even the saltpeter purchased and stored by the English Factors of the East India Company. The report deated 9th April, 1656 runs. "What Saltpeter was upon the ground when news arrived of Sadula C Kawnes death, the *Gomors* carried away."

74. Jahangir (vide *Tuzuk*, tr. Rodgers, p. 251) while narrating the expedition against the '*Gunwars*' near Mathura (*op. cit.*) in the 18th R.Y. States that, " numbers of them were killed, their women and children taken captive and a great booty acquired by the victorious troops" *Mahzar-i-Shahjahani*, pp. 10-11 states that in the 15th R.Y. of Jahangir's reign, the *Faujdar's* son pillaged the insurgent the people of Samejeh with tribal sub-division of Rajyal and Bhan in the *Pargana* of Darbela (*Sarkar* Bhakkar) and, "having

murdered many of these, imprisoned their children and wives and broguth them to the fort of Bhakkar." Also pp. 40-42. Similarly, *The English Factories* (*Ibid*) narrate the punitive measure against the '*Gomors*' near Agra and comment. "But it proved to their destruction; for they were suddenly surpised by Abdall Nubby (Abdul Nabhi) his (Sadullah Khan's) *Fauzdarr* (*Faujdar*) their towns sacked, and such as escaped not only by flight either slain or imprisoned."

75. *A.N.* Br. M. Add 257, 247 fol 332a, Ms. O.R. 26, 207 fol. 162a in its 27th year reforms vide clause 6th gives general instructions for the chastisement of the recalcitrant cultivators. The clause runs, " such of the turbulents who take shelter in a jungle or fort or a trench and do not pay the assessed revenue and rather damaged the *ryots* of the surrounding villages, the *Jagirdar* and the *Karori* of every *Subah* and every *Pargana* should for the protection of the *Raiya* (revenue paying subjects) warn the recalcitrants and the rioteous and demand from them the compensation for the damaged done to the *ryots*. First, they should admonish the recalcitrants and if the latter do not come around, the *Faujdar, Jagirdar* and the *Karori* should cut the jungle, demolish the fort and the trenches, and should completely destroy their cultivated fields." Beveridge's translation, vide II pp. 563-64 is rather defective; also for Jahangir's reign, Baharistan tr. Borah, p. 776; for Shah Jahan's reign, *Maktubat-i khan Jahan* Br. M. fol 7a-7b; for Aurangzeb's reign, of the many available documents, see R.A.J. *Misc. Pers. Letters* reg. 326, dated 9th *Jamadi* II, 24th R.Y./1680 A.D.; *Vakil Report* reg 1262, dated 4th *Jamadi* I, 50th R.Y. 1118 A.H./13th August 1706 A.D.

76. *Ibid.* The same clause of *Akbar Nama* runs further. "If it be the *Jagir* land, the *Diwans* should allot him an additional salary in lieu of the crop damaged and in case of a *Khalsa* land, the *Mustifis* should allow the *Karoris* due compensation……for the villages desolated by the recalcitrants, the *Mustifs* should not demand the shortage in the realisation from the *Karori* for a season's crop to full one year and likewise the *Diwans* would give additional *Jagir* to the assignees for the same period's compensation."

77. In Shah Jahan's reign, Nawab Muzaffar Khan (Vide *Maktubat-i Khan Jahan*, Br. M. fols 7a-7b) reported that in *Chakla* Gwalior, he had not realised any revenues from the recalcitrant areas in *Chakla* Gwalior for the last five years. Similarly, also for Aurangzeb's reign, R.A.J. '*Maharaja's Letters*' Reg no. 887, dated 40th R.Y. 1107 A.H.

78. *A.N.* Br. M.Add. 27, 247, fol 332; *Mufidul Insha*, fol 51b.

79. *Ibid. Mahzari Shahjahani*, pp. 6-8, 11, 37,38.

80. *Ibid. Mahzar-i Shah Jahani*, pp. 45-48 states that tribe of Daud Shora (*Sarkar* Chakar Hala, *Subah* Thatta) after reduction was settled on the newly formed lands of the river and thereafter became completely revenue paying.

81. R.A.J. *Shah Jahan's Farman*, no. 39/64, dated 5th R.Y. addressed to Raja Jai Singh for the suppression of the turbulents in the *Parganas* of Ruspur

and Nariana (*Subah* Ajmer) and to appoint new *Zamindars*; also R.A.J. category 2 reg 360 dated 37th R.Y./1693 A.D. Fidar Khan desires Hari Singh to send *Pai Kasht kars* (Cultivators) who may settle in his Jagir and pay the revenues regularly.

82. R.A.J. *Akhbarat*, Reg 361 23rd of Hurrah, 25th R.Y. 1092 A.H. /24th Nov. 1681 A.D.

83. *The English Factories* (1668-69), p. 228, Sarkar, '*Aurangzeb*' vol. V, pp. 116-117).

84. *Riyazul Vidad*, Br. M.O.R. 1725, fol 18; Also see *Risala-i Ansari* (Brochure by Ansaari) in *Majmua-i Munshiat*, Ms. Rampur, pp. 361-62 states the problems of the *Jagirdar* in the 29th and 30 R..Y. of Auranzeb consequent on the recalcitrant attitude of the *ryots*.

85. R.A.J. '*Maharaja's Letters*' reg no. 865 dated 39th R.Y. 1106 A.H. Also reg. 887 dated 40th R.Y. 1107 A.H.; *Vakil Report* reg no. 1262/95a dated 4th *Jamadi* I, 50th R.Y. 1118 A.H./1706 A.D. (for *Subah* Ajmer); *Original Letters* B.N. Paris No. (dealing with *Subah* Gujrat); *Letters of Nawish Khan*, Ms. Sarkar fols 8b-9b. Nawasish Khan, the *Faujdar* and *Qiladar* of Mandsor (*Subah M*alwa) wrote this letter to Prince Bedar Bakht, the Governor of Malwa; *Mufid ul Insha*, Ms. Fols 48b-49a, 51b. (dealing with Ghora Ghat, Cooch Bihar, *Subah* Bengal); *Durrululm* ms. Bod Oxford.

86. *Ibid.*, also *Insha-i Roshan Al Kulam* Ms. 1.0 no. 4011 417e fol 6b-8a 13a. (for Oudh, also see '*Chronicles of Oonao*' by C.A. Elliot, pp. 100-101, 117) shows the constant worries and operation of a *Faujadar* (about 1700 A.D.) against the recalcitrance of the *Zamindars, Riyazul-Vidad*, Ms. Br. M.fols 18a-18b, also Ms 873 Patna, notes the recalcitrant activities of the dragon-like *Zamindar* of Palampur, *Paragana* Chanwar (Chandwar vide *Ain*, J.II. p. 194 Ms. Oxford Br. M.O.R. 1725 fol 18a names it wrongly as *Jaju*) only 7 *krohs* from the city of Akbarabad, (Agra); Bernier, p. 208. Though Moreland (vide '*Agrarian System*', pp. 150-153) has rightly judged the fall in the *Jagir* income and its unpopularity by the close of the 17th century, he attributes it to the decline in the agricultural production and the weakening of the Central authority. His first argument of the fall in the agricultural production consequent on the scarcity and absconding of the peasantry (vide pp 144-5) as discussed later is unacceptable. His second argument of the decline of the central government is quie tenable but for want of any direct contemporary evidence for northern India after 1681 A.D. (As he himself concedes), he has not been able to analyse the problem deeper. Though with the growing lawlessness, agricultural production was bound to suffer, the main reason for the fall of an assignee income was the recalcitrance of the *Zamindars* who themselves pocketed the revenues of the territories assigned to the *Jagirdars*.

87. R.A.J. '*Maharaja' Letters*' Reg 865 dated 39th R.Y. 1106 A.H. A letter from Mohammad Hussain (*Diwan* of Ajmer) to the Maharaja (of Amber)

that Hari Ram, the latter's agent had plundered a village in the *Jagir* of Khallaq Ullah and having imprisoned the *Gumashtas* of the *Jagirdar* and had forcibly got written the lease deed (*Patta Ijara*) from the *Amil*. He had realised the revenues of the village in *Pargana* Halk amounting to Rs. 13000/- and having misappropriated Rs. 8000/- and returned only Rs. 5,000/- Another letter Reg 887 dated 40th R.Y. 1107 A.H. notes a complaint lodged to the *Diwan* of *Subah* Ajmer that Ruhr Singh who had been assigned *Jagir* in the *Parganas* of Halk and Asaf Abad had not been given the possession by the previous assignee. *Durululm* fol 48b-49a.

89. R.A.J. '*Maharaja's Letters*' case no. 627 dated 35th R.Y. 1103 A.H./1691 A.D. records a letter from Innayat Ullah Khan requests the Maharaja (of Amber) to direct the *Thanadar* of Bhasu to refund the *Peshkash* (10% of the revenue collections from his *Jagir* and that he had received a written complaint to this effect from the *Shiqdar, Qazi,* the *Muqaddams, Patwaries* and *Raiya* of his *Jagir*.

90. *Mufidul Insha*, fols 48b-49a, 52b-54b, 71a-74a. In Aurangzeb's reign, a *Mansabdar* was required to defray the expenditure of the rations (*Khurak wa Doab*) of the animals which rendered the assignee's position still more difficult. Also see Khwafi II, pp. 602-3, Moreland, p. 151.

91. *Ibid.*, R.A.J. *Vakil Report*, Reg 1262/95a dated 4th *Jamadi* I. 50th R.Y. 1118 A.H./1706 A.,D. states that Mansingh had a *Jagir* in *Subah* Akbarabad worth 330000 *dam* but had not been able to realise a single *dam* for the last six to seven years and that he likes to have his *Jagir* changed over to *Pargana* Kol in *Subah* Ajmer.

92. *Mufidul Insha*, fols 48-49; R.A.J. *Vakil Report, Ibid.*

93. *Ibid.*, fols 52b-54b; 77b-78b; R.A.J. *Vakil Report*, reg no. 369/239 dated 28th *Shaban* 34th R.Y. 1101 A.H./1690 A.D., also reg. no. 191/271 23rd *Shaban* 34th R.Y. 1102 A.H./1691 A.D.

94. Haft Anjman, *Letters of Rustam Khan to Jaffar Khan.*

95. *Letters of Nawish Khan*, Ms. Sarkar, fols 7a-9b. *Letter to Prince Bedar Bakht*, Governor of Malwa; *Risala-i Ansari* vide *Majmua-i Munshiat*, Ms. Rampur, fols 361-62.

96. *Durrul ulm*, fols 51a, 52b, 54b-55a, 56a, 62a;R.A.J.

97. *Ibid.* Also *Mufidul Insha*, fol 48b-49b, 51b.

98. *Mamuri*, Ms. Br. M. fols 157a, 177b; *Raqiam Kariam* Ms. Rampur, pp. 71-72, 157 vide *Aurangzeb's Letters to Prince Azim*; p. 176 Aurangzeb's order to *Mustifi* that no *Paibaqi* was left anywhere and that due to the desolation of the country and dishonesty of the *Amins*, no money reached the treasury and that in future assignments should be made in his presence; R.A.J. *Akhbarat*, dated 23rd of August, 1703 A.D. The Emperor issued an order that payments should be made in cash and that no Jagir assignment should be made to anybody without the orders of the Emperor.

99. R.A.J. *Akhbarat,* dated 13th Rabi I, 24 R.Y. states that the Emperor on consultation learnt from Ishetmad Khan *Diwan-i Tan* that there were abundance of *Paibaqi* lands.

100. Adab, *Aurangzeb's Letter to Shahjahan*, pp. 57-59.

101. *Selected Documents of Shahjahan,* pp. 109-113; 175-177.

102. Ahkam, pp. 71-72, 157, 176.

103. Zawabit Br. M.O.R. 1641, fol 15a; Sharma, *Mughal Government & Admininstration*, pp. iii-14. The number of *Mansabdars* had increased inordinately since Akbar's reign. According to *Ain*, (Blochmann I. p. 239), there were 1658 *Mansabdars* both *Jagirdars* and *Naqdi*, The number went up to 2069 in Jahangir's reign and 8,000 under Shahjahan (vide *Lahori* printed text, II, p. 715; Warris, MS. Rampur, p. 70 for 1659 A.D. also Sharma, *Mughal Government and Administration,* p. 110). Under Aurangzeb, in 1690 A.D., the number stood at 14,556 out of which 7667 were *Naqdi*, 6899 *Jagirdars* *Zawabit* Br. M.O.R. 1641, fol 15a; Ms. *Zawabit*, C.R.O. Hyd. puts the total at 14449. As the number of *Naqdis* and *Jagirdars* does not tally with the total number, evidently it is incorrect and the British Museum is more reliable). As such, the assignees numbered only 47.4% of the total *Mansabdars*. But the same ratio cannot be taken for the demarcation between the *Khalsa* and the *Jagir* lands as the high-ranking *Mansabdars* were invariably *Jagridars* holding large assignments.

104. *Ms. Sloane,* Br. M. 3582 (Sarkar's copy) pp. 59-64, 88-89, 63-64; also *Insha-i Kasim Tabsi,* R.A.S.B. No. 350, pp. 175-176.

105. Sarkar, Aurangzeb, vol. V, p. 68. Mir Jumla was enticed from the enemy camp and given a high *Mansab*. Also *Insha-i Khasim Tabsi*, p. 175; Ms. Sloane, pp. 61-62 states that in Karnatick all the previous religious grants and daily allowances were confirmed.

106. Ms. Sloane, pp. 63-64.

107. *Nuskha-i Dilkhusha* by Bhim Sen. Ms. Rieui 271; Or 23 fols 139a-140b.

108. *Ibid.*

109. Ankam, pp. 179-180

110. Khwafi, II, pp. 602-3. Khwafi Khan notes that even in Aurangzeb's reign, the *Jagir* situation had deteriorated. The situation was much worse when the author wrote in 1135 A.H./1722-23 A.D. Dr. Satish Chander's contention (vide '*Parties and Politics*' pp. introduction xvi-xvii, xi, iii-xivii) that the *Jagir* crises was due to the inability of the agricultural and industrial production to cope with increasing requirements of the ruling class is only partly true. In Mughal India, despite the growth of an affluent commerce and indigineous industry (vide Dr. Tara Chand's '*State and Society*', pp. 53-55. '*History of Freedom Movement*', pp. 172-84; Brij Narain, *Indian Economic Life*, pp. 25-27. In accordance with the medieval concept, the

burden of the expanding Mughal bureaucracy rested on the land revenue. The increase in the Mughal territories, its agricultural production and revenues could meet emoluements of the Mughal bureaucracy under more or less normal circumstances. But the socio-religious and political peculiarities of Aurangzeb's reign (See Adminsitration under Aurangzeb) having undermined the rule of law cut at the very source from which the revenues appropriated to the assigness flowed.

Index